THE FIRST
100 DAYS
OF YOUR BOOK

THE FIRST 100 DAYS OF YOUR BOOK

BOOK MARKETING FOR
SELF-PUBLISHED AUTHORS

JOEL STAFFORD

ISBN: 1690959150
ISBN-13: 978-1690959151

Website:
www.Joelbooks.com

Facebook page facebook.com/joelsbooks
Instagram page instagram.com/joelsbooks

First edition: September 2019
Updated: September 2020

TABLE OF CONTENTS

BEFORE THE D-DAY — 1
DAY -120 — 1
- GENERAL COMMENT — 1
- YOUR BOOK'S SUBTITLE — 1
- COVER — 2

DAY -90 — 4
- KDP — 4

DAY -70 — 6
- A KIND "END BOOK" MESSAGE — 6

DAY -65 — 7
- SOCIAL MEDIA — 7

DAY -60 — 8
- WEBSITE — 8

DAY -16 — 11
- KDP — 11

DAY -15 — 12
- KDP — 12

DAY -2 — 12
- KDP — 12

DAY -1 — 13
- KDP — 13

THE FIRST TWO WEEKS DAY 1-14 — 15
DAY 1 — 15
- GENERAL COMMENT — 15
- KDP — 15
- INSTAGRAM (IG) — 16

DAY 2 — 19
- FACEBOOK — 19
- TWITTER — 21
- LINKEDIN — 21

MARKETING CREATIVE	21
SHORT VIDEO	24
DAY 3	**24**
GENERAL COMMENT	24
GOODREADS	25
GOODREADS REVIEWS	26
GOODREADS LISTOPIA LISTS	26
DAY 4	**27**
LIBRARYTHING	27
BOOKBUB AND OTHER CATALOGUES	28
AMAZON AUTHOR CENTRAL	28
DAY 5	**29**
MARKETING MESSAGE	29
INSTAGRAM, PINTEREST, FACEBOOK, TWITTER, LINKEDIN	30
DAY 6	**31**
FACEBOOK GROUPS	31
DAY 7	**32**
GENERAL COMMENT – REST DAY	32
DAY 8	**33**
INFLUENCERS	33
DAY 9	**37**
WEBSITE SEO	37
DAY 10	**39**
PRESS RELEASE	39
DAY 11	**41**
WEBSITE CONTENT	41
DAY 12	**42**
ADVERTISING GENERAL	42
PREMIUM BOOK SITES	44
DAY 13	**47**
WEBSITE MEDIA KIT	47
DAY 14	**49**
GENERAL COMMENT – REST DAY	49
THE SECOND TWO WEEKS DAY 15-30	**51**
DAY 15	**51**
AMAZON ADS KEYWORD RESEARCH	51
DAY 16	**54**
AMAZON ADS	54

DAY 17	61
FACEBOOK GROUPS FOLLOW UP	61
DAY 18	63
INFLUENCERS FOLLOW UP	63
DAY 19	64
GOODREADS SELF-SERVE ADVERTISING	64
GENERAL COMMENT	65
QUORA ADS	66
DAY 20	67
PINTEREST ADS	67
DAY 21	69
GENERAL COMMENT – REST DAY	69
DAY 22	69
AMAZON ADS BID REVIEW	69
DAY 23	73
EMAIL MARKETING	73
DAY 24	75
BOOK AWARDS	75
DAY 25	77
AMAZON PAGE	77
DAY 26	79
SOCIAL MEDIA AND SIGNITURE	79
DAY 27	80
INSTAGRAM	80
DAY 28	81
GENERAL COMMENT – REST DAY	81
DAY 29	82
INFLUENCERS FOLLOW UP	82
DAY 30	83
AMAZON ADVERTISING	83
THE SECOND MONTH DAY 31-62	**87**
DAY 31-38	87
KINDLE COUNTDOWN DEALS (KCD)	87
FREE BOOK PROMOTION (FBP)	88
DAY 39-46	89
QUORA	89
DAY 47-54	91

REDDIT	91
DAY 55-62	**94**
TIKTOK	94
AMAZON ADS FOLLOW UP	94
THE THIRD MONTH AND BEYOND DAY 63-100	**97**
DAY 63-70	**97**
GOODREADS GIVEAWAY	97
DAY 71-78	**98**
INTERNATIONAL BOOK FAIRS	98
DAY 79-86	**105**
SEND YOUR BOOK FOR FREE IF REQUESTED	105
DAY 87-94	**106**
GENERAL COMMENT	106
DAY 95-100	**108**
THE CHECKLIST	108
SUMMARIZING 3 YEARS OF MARKETING EXPERIENCE	**111**
COMMON MISTAKES RELATED TO BOOKS	**112**
Cover	112
Amazon blurb and title	114
Pricing strategy	116
Length of the book	123
the importance of pre-order state	124
COMMON MISTAKES RELATED TO ADVERTISING	**126**
Unrealistic expectations	126
Amazon Ads	128
Quality of marketing visuals	131
Book genres	133
SUMMARY	**137**

QUICK MARKETING CHECKLIST

- ☐ Short but strong title, with subtitle including the book's keywords
- ☐ Compelling, quality cover
- ☐ Well written Amazon description
- ☐ Editorial reviews
- ☐ From author section on Amazon
- ☐ Amazon Author profile with relevant bio and profile picture
- ☐ Kind end book message to leave feedback on Amazon
- ☐ List your book on Goodreads
- ☐ List your book on Bookbub
- ☐ List your book on multiple Goodreads' Listopia lists
- ☐ Create a real photo about your paperback or Kindle book
- ☐ Linking your book to social media profiles (Facebook, Twitter, LinkedIn, Quora, Instagram, TikTok etc.)
- ☐ Put your new book into sticky post on your social media (Facebook, Twitter etc.)
- ☐ First Kindle Free or Countdown promotion

RESOURCES

Kindle Direct Publishing (KDP) merged with CreateSpace in 2018
https://kdp.amazon.com

Kindle Sales Reports (KDP)
https://kdpreports.amazon.com/sales

Amazon Advertising Platform (Amazon Self-Serve Ad Network)
https://advertising.amazon.com

Amazon Ads Campaign List (Amazon Ads)
https://advertising.amazon.com/cm/campaigns

Not allowed book genres in Amazon Ads
https://advertising.amazon.com/resources/ad-policy/creative-acceptance

Amazon Associates (Amazon Affiliate program)
https://affiliate-program.amazon.com

Amazon Author Central (adjusting book listing)
https://authorcentral.amazon.com

Goodreads (book catalogue)
https://www.goodreads.com

Listopia (Goodreads Listopia lists)
https://www.goodreads.com/list

Librarything (book catalogue)
https://www.librarything.com

Riffle (book catalogue)
https://www.rifflebooks.com

Libib (book catalogue)
https://www.libib.com

Delicious Library 3 (book catalogue)
https://www.delicious-monster.com

Anobii (book catalogue)
https://www.anobii.com

BookBrowse (book catalogue)
https://www.bookbrowse.com

Bookbub (book catalogue)
https://www.bookbub.com

Bargain Booksy (book promotional site)
https://www.bargainbooksy.com

BookSends (Kindle promotional site)
https://booksends.com

Joelbooks (book promotional site)
https://joelbooks.com

1618 Words (book promotional site)
https://1618words.com

Dr Mel's Message (book promotional site)
https://www.drmelmessage.com

Linktree (Instagram profile linking)
https://linktr.ee

Bitly (social media links)
https://bitly.com

Later (social media posting)
https://later.com

Buffer (social media posting)
https://buffer.com

Copyscape (checking plagiarism)
https://www.copyscape.com

Google Search Console (manually crawl new content on your site)
https://search.google.com/search-console

Keywords Everywhere (Amazon keyword research)
https://keywordseverywhere.com

Amazon Ads visual guide (setup your first Amazon Advertising)
https://joelbooks.com/amazon-advertising-guide

Goodreads Giveaways (giveaway platform)
https://www.goodreads.com/giveaway/show_create_options

Quora Advertising (advertising platform)
https://www.quora.com/business

Pinterest Advertising (advertising platform)
https://ads.pinterest.com

Reddit Ads (advertising platform)
https://ads.reddit.com

Mailchimp (email marketing platforms)
https://mailchimp.com

SendGrid (email marketing platforms)
https://sendgrid.com

AWeber (email marketing platforms)
https://www.aweber.com

99designs (professional book cover)
https://99designs.com

Fiverr (micro services)
https://www.fiverr.com

Updated on **09.07.2020**

BEFORE THE D-DAY

DAY -120

GENERAL COMMENT

First off, be aware that any marketing activity before publishing your book will reduce the time you could spend actually writing your book! So, before your book is released, don't spend your time and money on marketing! Don't blog, and don't research potential reviewers. I know you have limited resources, so spend them wisely - on creating your book. Make it your best, and create something truly excellent. Following my before "D-Day" timeline (publishing date) is essential. For example, creating a website is a time-consuming activity and is not a priority, you have more important goals to accomplish first.

YOUR BOOK'S SUBTITLE

You already gave your book a title or at least a working title. Now it's time to add a subtitle that will appear next to the main title of your Amazon book's listing.

DAY -120

Be sure to include some relevant keywords in your subtitle. For instance, if you are writing a book about Python programming, use a short and distinctive (unique) main title for your book, then add "Python programming for beginners" as a subtitle, for SEO reasons (we will talk more about SEO later, but in a nutshell, it helps visitors to find your book more easily).

COVER

The cover is an essential part of marketing. **We should admit, people judge your book by its cover**. Your cover shouldn't tell the whole story, but it should give potential readers a feeling of what it's about.

The cover should be of a professional standard. Based on my six years experience, 50% of the books have unprofessional covers and a further 20% of the books have covers which shouldn't be covers at all! According to UNESCO, approximately 2,200,000 books will be released in 2020. This means that 400,000 new books won't have any chance on the market, and more than 1,000,000 titles will be at a substantial disadvantage. The most shocking thing is that all of this is decided before the reader sees a single word of your story! No matter how good your story is, the cover can make or break its success. In the case of books what is called a "long tail effect" will occur, meaning that 20% of your books make

80% of your sales. If you start writing a book, you want to be in that 20%. So, suffice it to say, you need a professional cover.

Hire a good book cover designer (from a website like 99designs or Fiverr). Outsourcing this is something you should really consider. A good book cover is somewhere between $80-300. Whilst it may be tempting to underspend here, it's worth remembering that you get what you pay for and so for $10 you will most likely receive unprofessional work. Even if you are paying more, it is important to check the references/reviews of the designer and prepare a good summary of your story to give them to base their design on.

The first thing you should decide on is the length (in pages) of your book since it decides the spine width and the overall dimensions of your book when printed. There are several options available on the Kindle Direct Publishing platform, but not all trim sizes are accepted for Expanded Distribution. One of the most common book sizes is 5" x 8", with cream paper.

It is also important to remember, that for the next step (setting up pre-order) you will only need the front cover of your book. So, when you negotiate the timing with the designer always schedule a partial delivery for the front design. A reasonable time frame is within 1-2 weeks (after he or she starts the work).

DAY -90

KDP

Make your book's Kindle version available for pre-order on the Kindle Direct Publishing platform (KDP). The KDP platform allows you to make your book available for pre-order three months before the release date, all you need is a cover, book title, and a blurb. I know it is hard to decide on a definite release date for your book, but it is important. Not because you could start marketing your book before the release, but it will allow you to redirect people to the book's first landing page. You could refer to that page when you are speaking about your upcoming book to your friends or strangers.

People will find your book based on the title. When selecting a title, always choose a unique one, with less than four words so it is easy for people to remember. The subtitle can be longer, and it may contain topic keywords, especially if it is a non-fiction book.

The blurb, or short description of your book, should be catchy. Perhaps ask a friend for help and list out some words about your book to them, then ask him or her, what is the one detail, he or she remembered most clearly. People often find less important details more interesting than the thrilling parts of your book you might assume they would remember. Sometimes it could be a date, a setting, or an uncommon word, but a simple easy to remember detail will be it in most cases. As the writer who created the plot, it is often very hard to pick up on these words, this is why a friend or a professional beta reader can be extremely useful.

The pricing of your book is important. Remember, the bestselling Kindle books have a price under $5, but you want to receive 70% of the royalties and be enrolled in KDP select. This requires your book to be priced at $2.99 or more. The ideal initial price of your Kindle book should be between $2.99-$4.99, that is if you are between 100-300 pages in length. If your book is over 300 pages you should consider a higher price, or breaking it up into a series of smaller books.

DAY -70

A KIND "END BOOK" MESSAGE

You are most likely close to finishing your book's manuscript. This is the time when a good 'thank you for reading' message could be added at the end of the book.

Be honest with the readers; today we couldn't bypass the importance of reviews. Every new review could mean hundreds of new readers to your book, simply because of Amazon's ranking system. Adding a kind request at the end of your book is a painless way to improve your Amazon page with feedback.

If you want to get a further idea of what I am talking about, just go at the end of this book for a moment.

Some bookstagrammers also recommend putting a direct link or QR code in order to easily reach the review page of your book. Nobody likes searching for links, which is completely understandable.

No matter if we receive a good or bad review, these are just opinions. Welcome all of them! Think about well-written bestsellers. You won't find any typo, they are well researched and excellent in style- but guess what? They have a lot of 1-star reviews. Just giving a concrete example, the first Harry Potter book has currently up to

250 one-star reviews, which is 2% of all feedbacks. So once again in case of reviews, we focus on the mass and not on the quality.

DAY -65

SOCIAL MEDIA

You need to claim your Facebook, Instagram, Twitter, and Pinterest page names. Since these names are unique it could easily be the case that they are already taken. From this point of view, you have a **branding problem**. You need to establish an easily found and unique brand, which could originate from:

- your author-name
- your book's title
- series name

No matter which one you choose, you should keep it short and use it consistently. "Short" here means no more than three small and easy to remember words and "consistent usage" means it must be the same on each platform. I would recommend you start with an available .com domain name (you can check it's availability at Godaddy), then check the word on Facebook, Twitter, Instagram, and Pinterest.

DAY -60

What do you want to avoid when selecting a brand name?

Avoid using _ (underline), instead, write the words together.

If you really want to separate them, you may use - (hyphen), but only once, two hyphens in a brand name are overwhelming.

Avoid using **more than one number** in any title

Once you find the right name, claim it on every platform, even if you don't plan to use it! In the following years, it may come in handy!

DAY -60

WEBSITE

People often underestimate the value of web presence; that is to say, increasing your chances of being found on the web. No, it doesn't happen randomly when you set up a website. You need to put in the work to help search engines find it. Every person who is searching for terms like those that are included in your book or its title will then have a higher chance of finding your book. They may not know a damn thing about your book, but he or she has a clear picture of what they want to read and now your book is in front of them and seems to meet those criteria! This is where **keywords** come in. Whether you like it or not, your job is to list those keywords in a human and readable context, not just list them out in a long string.

The blurb of your Amazon book is more like a catchy collection of sentences, kind of like a brochure or a one-page website. It achieves the following:

1. Allows search engines (Google) to find your website
2. Prompts engines (Google) to put your website in a higher position in their search results
3. Redirects visitors to your book's Amazon page (Sales page)

The hardest task is definitely the second. It is called SEO. You can spend hundreds of dollars on buying SEO services in order to gain your website some authority, and possibly climb up a few positions in search results. But since this book isn't specifically about SEO, I just want to give you a few hints about where to start. Below are several SEO communities that you can join to learn more, and such forums are essentially the big brothers of SEO:

DAY -60

- Warrior Forum
- Black Hat World
- Wicked Fire
- Digital Point
- Reddit (SEO section)

Now back to the website, what you need to set up one in a day:

1. **Domain name** (Godaddy, Namecheap) choose a .com domain
2. **Hosting partner** (Hostgator, Webhostinghub)
3. **Blog engine** (Wordpress)
4. **Theme** (skin) **for your blog** (Jupiter, Elegant Themes, Jevelin)

A basic custom website costs between $300-500 (including developer work, first-year domain fees, hosting, and a theme). It is a fairly high investment for a single self-published book and this is why I usually recommend starting with a basic author website and listing all of your books there.

With this marketing option, you're shooting for long term marketing. It probably won't make any significant change in book sales in the first year (don't forget even with successful SEO, it can take years to find that search engine traffic).

So why is it worth it? In three to five years' time, you may get that all-important **free search engine traffic that** you deserve.

If you aren't a web developer I recommend you hire somebody to set up the whole website. It usually takes some time, often up to **30 days** to finalize it.

There are almost always free alternatives to creating a website manually, like Wix or Duda.co, which could work, but you would be dependent on a platform and you would never have full control of design or content.

DAY -16

KDP

Upload your final, edited manuscript and the paperback cover to KDP. At this point, your book should be ready to print. It takes approximately 1 day for Amazon KDP staff to review your cover and interior, then another 5-14 days to print and send a physical copy to you. Don't release it to the public, KDP has an option to order review copies before the release.

At this point just upload it and start the review process. No spelling or editing errors should be in the

DAY -15

PDF file at this point (though you will most likely find some anyway, no matter how sure you are!).

This will be the pre-launch edition of your book, which shouldn't be shown to anyone. Don't use this version as an ARC copy, only use it to help you in "debugging" your final manuscript.

DAY -15

KDP

Order one physical copy of your book. In the meantime, you should turn the error-finding mode on. Trust me, your book will never be perfect, but the more errors and mistakes you correct, the most likely your book will be to stand out from the crowd.

DAY -2

KDP

Once you received the physical copy, you could fix formatting errors, such as "that line spacing is too much" or "that title should be bigger" etc.

DAY -1

KDP

Close the first edition, save your edited word file into "print-ready PDF" and upload it to KDP. This new version will be available the next day. This could be the first ARC (Advanced Reading Copy) of your book. If you have a different cover for your ARC don't forget to upload it along with the final PDF.

THE FIRST TWO WEEKS
DAY 1-14

DAY 1

GENERAL COMMENT

This is the very first day of your book and your first day as a published author. Enjoy the day! I would personally recommend avoiding any work at all on this day. You deserve a rest after months of hard work putting the book together.

But on the other hand, I'm also a professional, so I would stay on top of certain things and important points that should be done on the first day.

Your book is a newborn. The publication date will be important later on since you could stick with this date to launch anniversary promotions. So, let's run through a few important things you can do now:

KDP

First off, order five copies of your physical book. Keep one copy for yourself and gave the others to your friends and family (don't forget to sign them!).

DAY 1

INSTAGRAM (IG)

Take a photo of your new book with your mobile (shouldn't be a professional one). It is a little bit tricky since you ordered five copies seconds ago, and even though Amazon delivery is fast, it is not as fast as to deliver it within 2 hours. But don't forget you ordered a review copy for error correction. This is why it was important to finalize the cover of your book months ago, before the actual release, so now you can feel confident taking photos of it!

Hold it in your hand and ask a friend to shoot some clear pics (high quality is really important). If you are too shy, you can also put the book on a nice table (either modern or vintage) with some fancy stuff and good lighting. Something to remember is that the book cover should be in the center and more or less directly in front of the camera. Avoid direct sunshine or dark places.

Save photos in your "Marketing" library, keep them in order, since there will be a lot of marketing materials later on.

Upload to your already existing Instagram account. And how should you format your post? Let's see:

- Use primary genre hashtags like #sciencefiction, #businessbooks, #romancebooks etc. (you can

check these hashtags by writing them into the Instagram search field) use them at the beginning of the post and limit to 2-3 maximum
- Write 2 lines about your story, like *"An 80-year-old soldier discovers a secret about his life, in a place where he didn't expect it at all."*
- Write where the book is available like *"Available now on Amazon."*
- Now put all of the other keywords you found at the end of the post, at least 5-10 of them, the more specific you are the more likely the crowd will come across your book, so keywords like "butterflystories" are good, which has 2,000-10,000 posts.
- Don't forget to mention people on Instagram with @ if somebody contributed to your book, or you simply want to say *"Thank You!"*

Keywording on social media is an art, but as you can see there are some simple rules. Another thing to focus your attention on is that I didn't mention Facebook. Don't post your book to any of your pre-existing Facebook pages on the first day.

Also, don't use a filter on IG! Keep the photo natural, but if you want to pump it up, go to photoshop and use a simple auto-correction option like "Image / Auto tone" or, my favorite; "Image / Adjustments / Match Color".

DAY 1

There are several good applications on Android and iPhone which could also be used to make some professional adjustments like Afterlight, Aviary, or Snapseed, but again keep the natural feeling of the photo.

You want to post this to a new author IG account, or even a separate account dedicated to only that book, especially if it will be a series.

If you have a personal profile on IG you can also post your book there - just forget about keywording and write an honest personal message to your friends. Also, don't forget to tell them where the book is available. Several authors forget to tell their friends where their work can be bought. Be straight with them- friends will be your primary fan club and they will probably be interested in buying your book if you show them where to do it!

In the case of IG you shouldn't put any links to your book in your post. Don't even try it. People can't easily copy/paste from IG, so if you just write "The book is available on Amazon.com" it will be enough. Putting any links to the post will just mess it up. **Instagram stopped linking sites several years ago**.

So what else can you do? Put a link into your profile, every IG page has a profile link at the top. If you have more than one website, use services like Linktree.

Always use direct links to your book's Amazon page. Most people will prefer the paperback version of your book so use that link in the first place.

DAY 2

FACEBOOK

If you're probably wondering why I didn't mention posting your first photo on any other social media on Day 1, the reason is simple. A single post isn't as valuable as the responses it generates. **Answer all of the comments from Day 1.** Even thank the people who sent you likes on Instagram. The conversation is important, as later all of the **third party visitors will see these comments** and they will form a picture about this book and you as an author. Healthy engagement can result in sales, keep that in mind! So engaging with the audience is almost as important as the post itself.

Start this day with Facebook. On Facebook, you can post only to the people who are in your network (this is also true of Twitter and LinkedIn). If you have 500 friends, only half of them will see your post, this also depends on how active you are on Facebook. If you have a page with 1,000 likes it is most likely that 10-40% of the people will see the post and almost certain that at least someone will see it. IG works much better in that respect, as on Facebook keywords are almost useless.

One thing you can do on Facebook, and later on Twitter, is to put links in the post. These platforms tolerate outbound links a bit more.

Now let's see the post:

- Upload the photo. It is important since the post should be an **image post** (not link post).
- Write 3-4 lines maximum about your book.
- Put your sales link in the post.
- Put extra line breaks before and after the link.
- Lastly, keywords (maybe it will be useful one day).

Facebook likes content but hates links that redirect out of Facebook. If you would like to increase the efficiency of your link, use link shorteners like Bitly. Another interesting thing you could try out is Amazon Affiliates. After registering on the site, you can pick up your social sites into the affiliate program and create short affiliate links from your paperback or Kindle URL using SiteStripe (an Amazon Affiliate toolbar). This way you can also measure the traffic over your affiliate links and if you have a successful book, you may also make money.

TWITTER

For Twitter, you can use the same type of post as on Facebook, just a little bit shorter. Put it out as a "Pinned Tweet." Don't forget to edit your profile:

- Enter your author or book website's link into your bio information.
- ~~Update the cover~~ (No, you can't do that now, since there is no suitable creative image for that)
- In your bio, you can write that you are "Author of [Your Book's Title"]

LINKEDIN

Once you are ready with your other social media, you can tackle LinkedIn. I would draw your attention to the fact that people care less (much less) about fictional books on LinkedIn as they do about non-fiction books.

LinkedIn has several active groups. Look for the relevant ones and feel free to post with the fact that you just released a new book in that topic, though be sure the group policy allows this. LinkedIn groups are more open in terms of marketing than Facebook groups.

MARKETING CREATIVE

As mentioned earlier, in the case of Twitter, we need to be more creative.

DAY 2

Most probably your cover's dimensions are 5.25" x 8" or 6" x 9"- these are portrait aspect ratios. I see a lot of authors who just upload their cover to Facebook. Don't do that; it looks terrible. Most of the social media platforms (except Pinterest) prefer landscape (Facebook, Twitter, LinkedIn) or square (Instagram) aspect ratios. Which basically means you have to put a background image behind your cover.

You may even want to convert your cover to 3D. Search for "free book mockups PSD" on Google and click the image of the one you like. You download the photoshop source file and place your flat front cover into the right container. Voilà, your 3D book front cover is ready!

The work doesn't stop here. You need to find a good background for your 3D book cover. It could be a table or any other environment that you feel is appropriate for your book. Put it in, adjust any shadows and you are ready. Just to give you an idea, here is a sample of how it should look:

You can of course outsource this design task to somebody on Fiverr or any other freelancer, and it should take a maximum of 2-3 days to receive the creative. Maybe it isn't 100% natural, but keep the following things in mind:

- The book should be in the center
- The book's title and the author's name should be easily readable
- The book shouldn't be grey or in shadow
- The colors on the book should be vibrant

Having such marketing creative is essential in later stages. An alternative (but more expensive) solution is to hire a professional photographer and order some professional pictures of your book. It takes more time,

DAY 3

but it is worth it, especially if you have a friend who is a photographer - it can't hurt to ask them!.

SHORT VIDEO

The popularity of short videos is rising. If you have a decent marketing budget you could order a promo video for book marketing. It is true that people are more likely to click on trailers to learn more about a book. But don't be naive; videos aren't almighty. If you simply upload it to an empty YouTube channel, or an almost unknown Facebook page it won't have any impact, no matter how many keywords you put in the description.

Creating a good quality video can cost up to $100, and don't spend a penny on low-quality service providers. Nobody will do a good job for $10.

DAY 3

GENERAL COMMENT

Okay. Preparing your creative requires several days if you can't do it single-handedly, so let's continue with something else.

I would like to point out one important thing. After several days your best friends may mention that they bought your book. First, thank them and secondly ask them to review your book on Amazon. It doesn't even matter if they give 4 or 5 stars, the only thing that matters is to **collect as many reviews as you can**! The same is true for Goodreads. Every review you collect increases the chance that people will try your book out. Bestseller books have up to 100 reviews or ratings, and the top 100 books on Amazon have over 1,000 reviews. First, aim to collect somewhere in the range of 10-20 reviews.

GOODREADS

Register for an account on Goodreads. If you already have one, register another. The one with your actual name will be your Goodreads Author account, the other will be a technical account.

With the technical account, submit your book to Goodreads:

1. Search for your book title on Goodreads
2. If you can't find your book, click "Manually add a book"
3. Enter all the details and upload your book's cover in high resolution

Now your Kindle or paperback book should appear on Goodreads. On Goodreads all of your book versions are handled separately. Decide which will be your primary

DAY 3

format (I prefer paperback). It is important because you share this link with everyone later on.

GOODREADS REVIEWS

For Amazon users, reviewing isn't a simple thing, since in most cases you have to buy the book from Amazon in order to review it. Even if you receive a borrowed book, it could be the case that the platform doesn't allow you to review it.

This isn't true for Goodreads. On Goodreads you can rate and review any book you ever read. This is why I recommend you ask for reviews from your friends primarily on Goodreads and, if possible, on Amazon too.

GOODREADS LISTOPIA LISTS

Another interesting opportunity on Goodreads is the Listopia feature. After you read a book you may add that book to these lists, unless it is your own book (Goodreads Authors aren't allowed to vote on their own work).

Use your technical account and mark your book as read. You should then give a rating. Now search for relevant Listopia lists for your book. There is no recommendation as far as numbers go, the more lists you find the better. Now vote the book into each list, so the book will receive

1-1 vote on each list and these lists will be listed after 3-5 days under the book's profile page on Goodreads. After that, others can easily find these and, more importantly, give a 1-1 vote.

The more votes your book receives the higher it will be placed on these lists.

There are high competition lists, where you need thousands of votes to be in the top 100, but there are low competition lists where your book needs only 3-4 votes to get into the top 10. Topic-specific lists are usually low competition lists, so it is worth it to find these ultra-specific lists.

DAY 4

LIBRARYTHING

Goodreads may be the most famous book catalogue out there, but there are also alternatives for listing. One of the best ones is *Librarything*.

The listing works more or less the same in the case of all catalogues.

BOOKBUB AND OTHER CATALOGUES

There are several catalogues which are also worth listing your book in, they are all free:

- Listal
- Bookbub
- Libib
- Litsy
- Anobii
- BookBrowse

AMAZON AUTHOR CENTRAL

Now we are done listing our book on other sites we should also check our author profile on Amazon by visiting Amazon Author Central.

- Upload your author photo
- Write a proper biography
- Under Books, add your new work to the list (this way Amazon will list all of your books under your author profile)

Amazon Author Central has several useful features like allowing you to see all of the reviews on Amazon in one place and displaying your Amazon Bestseller Rank.

Though, if you are looking for sales numbers, I would recommend Kindle Sales Reports, as it is more colourful and accurate.

DAY 5

MARKETING MESSAGE

We haven't particularly focused on your marketing message yet. Now is the time. When you wrote your first posts on social media about your book, you most likely shared a tiny summary of your book and perhaps an excerpt with a few sentences. It is hard to catch the potential reader's attention with a story summary. Why? Because there are over 2,000,000 books published every year and, believe it or not, there are a lot of commonalities within those stories, with a lot of stories starting a kingdom, in a local village, or even on a space station. Writing just a few lines about your story won't have a clickbait effect.

Most of the authors forget that readers are not only interested in the story, but the author behind the story! Show your readers your intention, why **you** wrote this book in the first place? It can be an even stronger marketing message than the story itself. Express why this story is important to you!

DAY 5

INSTAGRAM, PINTEREST, FACEBOOK, TWITTER, LINKEDIN

Time to post again. At this time, you will need your **new portrait creative** with a background, or a promo video. Either way, you should prepare a new message for followers.

I usually post with some third-party apps to social media. For Pinterest and Instagram, I prefer **Later** and I use **Buffer** for the rest.

This time you can use the same text for each of them, but be creative! Maybe you could try some new keywords. Remember, you can also use keywords on Pinterest. Pinterest is a strong platform that may lead some visitors to your book.

Your post should contain:

- Message to the readers
- Where your book is available (direct link if possible to Amazon)
- Hashtags

In the case of Instagram, you want to crop your creative to be square, but remember don't use any filter.

DAY 6

FACEBOOK GROUPS

I mentioned there are a lot of Facebook groups containing up to 10,000 followers, that are focused on book marketing. On Fiverr I see a lot of guys who are actually promoting that they will share your book in these groups, claiming that they will share your book with "Up to 100,000 readers".

The truth is these groups just don't work. To give you a clue about what I'm referencing here, watch out for groups like:

- "Promote Your Book Here"
- "FREE Kindle Book Promotion"
- "Great books to read"
- "Authors promote your books"

There are a lot of people in these groups, so why doesn't it work? Simple: because the members are also authors!

If I was a reader would search terms into Facebook like:

- "2020 space marine sci-fi books"
- "newly released medieval romance novel"

Think like a reader. The groups you find this way may have lower member numbers, but the only numbers you

DAY 7

should check are the like and comment numbers under the post. If it has less than 3-4 engagements per post, then the group is an inactive group, and not worth your time.

Though there are good Facebook groups and communities that you can join for free, based on my experiences posting in these active groups a book on the same topic costs money and you should attempt to connect directly with the group administrator.

By this point, you should be looking to join at least a few of these closed groups. Aim to join at least 5-10 groups, which are all closely connected to your book genre. In one or two weeks you should post your news -that you wrote a book on this topic! The key is to remain polite in every interaction, if possible even contact the admin first and ask whether promoting books is allowed.

DAY 7

GENERAL COMMENT – REST DAY

Have a rest. You are a human being, after all. Enjoy the day! This was the first week of your new book.

DAY 8

INFLUENCERS

There are two types of influencers in the world of books:

1. **Individual readers** (they have an Instagram account)
2. **Book sites, book club owners** (they have a .com website)

Both of them are good to market our book. The negotiation is time-consuming and may cost money (at least the paperback book you will send to them) but it is worth it.

First, let's start with individual influencers.

Based on my experiences they are all book nerds and good guys. They normally read all the books they pick. They have limited time resources though, which makes the process really tricky.

There are several unwritten rules of contacting an Influencer:

- Never ask to review your book for free – Just because somebody is a book nerd doesn't mean she will buy your book. You may ask the

Influencer for their time, and not the rating you receive.
- Never ask for better rating – If your book isn't enjoyed by the influencer it may receive a lower rating- don't complain! A negative rating is still better than a book with absolutely no ratings.
- You need to send a paperback book to the influencer, plus a fixed fee for his or her time – this is the standard and I must say it's reasonable. Check the Influencer's social media. How many people does he or she reach and how many people respond to his or her posts?

Ok, now back to the task at hand:

1. Find influencers in your book's niche
2. Create a list before contacting anybody
3. Create a short message which you will use for contacting them
4. Finally, send out your messages

How to find the right Influencers?

Goodreads

Goodreads is an excellent way to find influencers, and the process is very straightforward:

DAY 8

1. Look up some popular books in the same genre as yours.
2. Go to reviews and search for reviews starting with "received the book for an honest review."
3. Check their profile and search for contact options and social media. The best amateur influencers have a social media following base somewhere between 1,000-9,000 followers.
4. Save their link, or try to add them as a friend to your Goodreads account with a friendly message.

Instagram

1. Enter hashtags of your book (like "#romancebooks", "#readromance").
2. Search for popular posts that contain a single book title.
3. Check the person who shared it (filter those who are individuals).
4. Check the other posts on the person's profile, if there are any book shares and they have up to 1,500 followers, then bingo!
5. Save their link and try to find their contact information.

Try to find 10-20 influencers. Befriend profiles with up to 10,000 followers and also profiles with lower numbers

DAY 8

in the range of 1,000-2,000 followers. Filter those whose posts don't have any likes. You want to find profiles that have active follower bases.

Influencer websites

You may try to find influencers on websites or collecting sites like influence.co, which is a good idea. It is also a good idea to save only relevant influencers who do actually read your genre.

After you have prepared the contact message, send it to them, and be transparent:

- Include your book's link.
- Be clear. You will provide the book (send a paperback copy to him or her).
- You will cover the fee for reading the book (if you have a budget indicate it here).
- What you want (review on Goodreads, website, and post on their social media).

Be friendly- they are all individuals and doing this in their free time! Never ask for positive reviews; you are approaching strangers, and you are also a stranger from their perspective. So, again, always ask for honest reviews!

Now send out the contact messages. You will most likely achieve a 20-40% response rate, which is normal in cold contacting via Goodreads or Instagram messages. There will be follow up tasks after this day.

On Day 12 we will continue with Book sites (Premium Book Sites).

DAY 9

WEBSITE SEO

As described on Day -60 you need some kind of website to establish a strong web presence in the long term. Either you outsourced the task or spent the time to create a new one yourself. Just remember to always ensure you own your own domain and brand of your website.

An optimal state to have reached at this point is when you can share www.myauthorname.com to everybody. Never use a subdomain for sharing purposes, only if it is your book's subpage like authorname.com/booksname or, a more elegant solution such as booksname.authorname.com. This is something you can do easily by visiting your domain name service provider (like Godaddy) and adding a new subdomain manually then redirect it to a page that already exists on your site. You can also mask it.

DAY 9

After you have a website you want search engines to find it, you have to order certain SEO services from professionals. Head to forum marketplaces like BHW forum and buy 1-2 complex packages for your site and be sure the package includes the following elements:

- Link building (Tier 1-2 sites, don't trust in mass link building on Tier 3-4 sites. It could even harm your website)
- Social media signals
- Posts on popular (high DA) websites
- Do follow backlinks from popular (high DA) websites

It will cost approximately $80-120; it isn't worth buying higher packages at this time. All you want is to get into the Google index.

Before ordering any packages, collect the most important 4-5 keywords that will be relevant to your site and book. Choose the keywords which best describe your book's content:

- "historical family saga"
- "military science fiction"
- "urban fantasy"

Never use top-level categories like "fantasy" or "romance" instead, always take the time to find more specific keywords.

DAY 10

PRESS RELEASE

This is something you want to outsource to professionals. Writing a press release is time-consuming and something which is difficult to do well yourself.

The key is what PR network provider you are working with. The most important thing is that your press release should be guaranteed to feature in Google News. This should be an expectation you have when paying $50-100 to a professional.

Keep in mind the message of the article is important; you just released a book. A professional writer will say: ok, and what? You need to share why this book release is important. This should be given to the article writer prior to placing the order.

Some reliable PR service provider:
- PRWeb
- PR Newswire

DAY 10

- eReleases
- BusinessWire
- PRLeap

A trick is that these service providers are also present in forums like BHW and you can secure a substantial discount if you order directly from individuals. So, visiting the service providers sites won't be the most cost-effective solution.

The press release is typically delivered within 7 days by the above providers. Once it is out you will receive a collection of the sites where the article is available.

In press releases, you can always link to your website which will increase the DA (Domain Authority) rank of the domain and improve the SEO of your website. In addition, you want to list the most important keywords in the article to help Google to connect your book's title with the keywords.

The big question is - how many sales can I achieve with a press release? How many visitors will be led to your book? The answer is most probably 0-3 sales, but a decent amount of traffic. It depends on the service provider you choose. One thing is for sure from a traffic point of view - it is not worth doing a press release, but it is really healthy from an SEO point of view.

When I worked with press releases it was really good when I had to refer to "official" sources about the book. Writing anything on your website will never be classified as official, but putting it out to the public is a big help and makes it feel like more of a big deal.

DAY 11

WEBSITE CONTENT

Writing content on your website is essential in 2020. You want to write at least three 1,000-1,500 word articles.

If you write fiction, then these could be short stories in the style of the book. Be as unique as you can be, and never copy/paste content from other websites. If you outsource article writing, always check the end result with Copyscape before posting to your site.

If you wrote a non-fiction book, then write articles connected to your book's topic. Alternatively, you can simply share news on your site, but it is important to provide unique content for site visitors.

In Google Search Console you can initiate a fresh Google indexing simply by entering the new content's URL to the search field, so Google will be aware of your new article. This will also happen automatically by Google, but it takes time (days to weeks) to re-crawl your whole site.

Generating and posting content on your site is the best way to climb to a higher position on Google.

DAY 12

ADVERTISING GENERAL

I haven't yet mentioned the different advertising platforms available on the market. Based on my own experiences, not every platform is suitable for independent book marketing.

Why? Because independent publishers haven't got a professional team behind who can plan and prepare all the necessary information and adjust the campaign performance on a daily basis. We need trade-offs here - a simple but effective platform that could be controlled by a single person, in our case the author.

Let's take a look at the alternatives:

1. Google Adwords
2. Facebook advertising
3. Amazon Advertising
4. Quora advertising

5. Pinterest Ads
6. Goodreads Self-Serve Advertising

As a beginner marketing specialist (years ago) I said, "I should start with the biggest one" (Google). I spent a lot of money on the platform for book marketing, created several ads and campaigns, but every campaign resulted in negative ROI (Return on Investment). First, I thought I was an idiot, but later I realized that there is huge competition on Google Ads. You need to highly optimize your ad presence and you need the necessary resources to do that.

In the case of Facebook ads, you receive impressions - this is the only platform where you pay after "engagements" which will not likely convert later to visits and sales. Every book ad which is effective on Facebook is more like a scam, and full of hidden facts: "Get this book for free." After clicking on the website of the author you realize there is a big postage fee, but basically the book itself is "free".

Facebook is struggling with its ads platform's effectiveness, and the situation got worse in 2020. Literally you see sponsored ads in positions 2, 6, 10, 14, 18 in your feed. 25% of the content you see on Facebook is an advertisement. As a book marketing specialist, I would say Facebook has one of the biggest cost-per-click fees among the big platforms.

Selling my book to an unknown person is a connection that is based on trust. The customer advances this trust to the author. With a bad ad, you could kill this trust instantly. So, always be honest with your campaign message!

Years later I came back to other forms of advertising and found that with the following two platforms you could achieve results with low expertise:

- **Amazon Ads**
- **Quora Advertising**

In a sense, they are easier to handle than Google or Facebook ads. In the following part of the book, we will be focusing on these two forms of paid advertising and I recommend that you avoid the other ones unless you have an expert friend who has a ton of experience.

PREMIUM BOOK SITES

Premium book sites are websites where you can list your book and potentially reach a unique audience. Most of these websites have some kind of freebies, but in most cases, they are specialized for promotional periods. For example, if you have a Kindle Countdown Deal for 5 days, you may want to spread the word, and here is where these websites come into the picture since they will promote your book during these days to their visitors, but in most cases, it will cost you a one time fee of somewhere between $10-200.

How to select the right site for you?

Think like a reader. 90% of these websites are really old school. They don't care much about design and that is a problem. Always pick websites that appear trustworthy from a reader's perspective. If you don't like the design, then avoid spending a penny!

Another consideration is that your book's genre should match the most popular genres of the website. Just to give you an idea, if you can't find any non-fiction books on their website, then don't try to promote yours. It is likely that your book won't receive any clicks because of genre mismatch.

Always check the social stats of the website; if you don't find likes, comments, or any reactions, it may have less than an optimal number of visitors or maybe even 0. Don't be fooled by words. Anyone can write on the website that they will put your book in front of 10,000 readers, but if these readers are not active on their social media then it is worth nothing to list your book. You are looking for reactions first.

DAY 12

In the following list, I tried to collect some of these websites.

- Bookbub – specialized for Kindle books, has great visitor numbers but isn't a cheap option.
- Freebooksy – specialized for free book promotions.
- Bargainbooksy – one popular book website which is useful if you have a Kindle Countdown promotion.
- Ereader News Today – they built up a nice audience over time, both on the website and social media.
- Joelbooks (this is our site) – an aspiring website started by our book club in 2018.

On most of these websites, you will find a "book submit form" where you can add payment details, usually Paypal. You may find tons of other premium book sites on sites such as the Kindlepreneur blog but be careful with these sites. I have heard a lot of stories where a new indie author paid up to $80 for zero visitors. I call these "zombie" websites.

Please note that these raw forms of marketing are impersonal in many ways in 2020, and won't work if you're trying to appeal to a younger audience unless the website is also active on Instagram, where these youngsters are present.

If you want to use this way of advertising always look for feedback from reliable sources, not just from the website itself as their sales copy is often misleading. Just to give you an idea, on Fiverr people need to submit feedback about services, so fake or low-quality services will be filtered out very quickly. If there is no third party option to validate a service, try to search for it on Twitter, Facebook, or Quora.

DAY 13

WEBSITE MEDIA KIT

It is always a good thing to promote your resources on your website. It helps to spread the word and it is really professional.

You create what is called a "media kit" on your website. This is what the media will use if they want to share a story or anything else about your book. They will look up your website and use resources found in the media kit.

These resources are mainly visual, but there should also be the following:

DAY 13

- Your book's front cover in high resolution
- The author's biography in PDF or plain text format (no formatting)
- Author's official portrait
- Official contact information (full name, email, social media links, website link, and your agent's name if applicable)
- A copy of your press release saved as a PDF and relevant links (1-2) to where it has been published
- More photographs of the author and/or the book
- Official visual ads (creatives) about your book (since your book is in portrait aspect ratio, this creative should be a landscape image. A lot of news sites prefer this over just a simple cover design, also please note this one is the same creatives that we prepared on Day 2)

Also, be sure to add a "last updated" date to the bottom of this site.

DAY 14

GENERAL COMMENT – REST DAY

OK, so it's been a tightly packed couple of weeks and we still haven't arrived at the most important part, but the above were essential first steps to have taken.

Book marketing is a tough thing because you will never experience any direct response or success even when the "big" marketing books suggest to "measure, measure, and measure." You simply can't connect sales to only one marketing action in real-time like this. Perhaps the sales were the result of a Facebook ad, but in reality, you will never know how many times the visitor saw your book, or where they came from before buying.

In the case of book marketing, we are working to get as many impressions as possible. It is said that we see a book ten times before we even consider buying it. I can relate to this simple argument.

This is why I suggest you work on long term marketing, as website owners work for SEO because after years people will still find their website. This is the effect we want your book to have too.

THE SECOND TWO WEEKS
DAY 15-30

DAY 15

AMAZON ADS KEYWORD RESEARCH

In the first days when we posted on social media, we did a small search for hashtags and keywords. If you are using any form of advertising keywords, then this is an essential tool for you. That is why we are focusing on this topic. Today's task is to create an Amazon keyword list, which we will use for Amazon Sponsored Product Advertising.

For quick help and more information on this, you should download *Keywords Everywhere's* plugin for your browser or *KDP Rocket*. This will help you have some clue about which individual keywords to select.

Open an excel or notepad document, where you will store these keywords.

How to start the research?

Broadly speaking, there are two types of keywords:

1. Genre specific or generic keywords

2. Ultra-specific keywords

Both of these keyword types have "long form."

Here are some examples in the case of a new romance book:

- Genre specific keyword: "romance books"
- Genre specific keyword, long form: "bestselling romance books"
- Ultra-specific keywords: "medieval romance"
- Ultra-specific keywords, long form: "medieval romance kindle books"

When I'm speaking about ultra-specific or ultra-relevant keywords, I mean keywords that have a search volume somewhere between 500-2,000. It brings lower, but more relevant traffic to your book, and these visitors are more likely to buy your book.

In contrast, generic keywords' search volume may by over 10,000 searches per month, but people entering these keywords are not 100% sure what they are searching for and so your book will have less chance of being bought.

If you want to run a low budget ad campaign on Amazon, use only ultra-relevant keywords. If you want to generate as many impressions as you can, you should use generic keywords.

DAY 15

If you think you have found a keyword, enter the term into Amazon and examine the results. It may be the case that not only books are appearing in the search result, as, don't forget, Amazon is also a marketplace for all kinds of consumer products.

The biggest product category is still books on Amazon, with more than 44.2 million titles in different forms. Categories like electronics also have similarly high numbers, with up to 10 million products, with home & kitchen and music comprised of a further 6 million products.

So, when you have keywords like "diet," always check them in search, because it could easily be the case that diet pills will appear in your search, and not books as you would normally expect. Please note that this is why nutrition and diet books have a hard time competing with pills and nutritional supplements.

An alternative keyword research strategy is finding your competitors and looking for keywords in their title or blurb (Subtitles of books are often used for storing relevant keywords).

Now that we have a bunch of keywords in our list, only filter "0 search keywords," which is to say keywords that nobody writes in the search field. You can easily check this with the above keywords tool.

DAY 16

AMAZON ADS

I had a long conversation in 2020 about the effectiveness of Amazon Ads. In 2019 the ad platform delivered decent results, but in 2020 since the beginning of the COVID-19 crisis, the results are really bad, which means negative ROI in practice, in the case of 40-60% of new campaigns. Amazon constantly modifies the placement of ads; for example, at the time I wrote these lines, you would find **six** sponsored product ads on the first page of Amazon search results (two on the top, two in the middle, and two at the bottom). Too many advertised products will lead to less effective ads. Maybe this is what we experience in 2020.

In this situation, your first question should be "which books are working with Amazon Ads?" Overall niche-specific non-fiction books are at an advantage. Just to give you some ideas:

- Python programming (IT-related books)
- History books
- Higher Education

In the case of fiction books, the effectiveness is lower, but if you could find your exact subgenre, it is almost a half win. If you write science fiction, and the story is about time travel, then I would target only time travel sci-fi related keywords. Not science fiction itself.

How can I set up my first Amazon Ads campaign?

If you've never used Amazon Advertising, you need to start with your account. Amazon's self-service platform requires you to have a Seller, Vendor, Advantage Central, or **KDP account**. The last one is what I will be talking about here.

The easiest way to register is to follow the links from your KDP account:

- Under your books, click on "Promote and Advertise"
- On the next page search and click on "Create an ad campaign"
- Select the appropriate marketplace you would like to promote (like amazon.com)
- This will redirect to Amazon Advertising platform

I've also prepared a quick Amazon Ads visual guide to help you (find the link in resources).

When setting up your first ad campaign you want to set up a Sponsored Products ad. There are other options (like Lock screen Ads) but these options are for mass marketing and they aren't worth it to try out as an

DAY 16

individual author (I tried Lock Screen Ads and discovered they have negative ROI, in 2019).

On the campaign setup page, you can change several settings like:

- Daily budget (if you want to maximize spending)
- Standard or custom text ad (both can be good)
- Always select manual targeting keywords (you want to control what happens with your ad)
- Select the format where you receive a higher cut of royalties (you pay advertising fees from your royalty. Make sure you redirect people to the product where you stand to receive more royalties per sale - try out KDP Royalty Calculator to see which one this is)
- Select keyword targeting first (later you can try product targeting); this is the place where we need to enter all of the keywords, we found yesterday
- Adjust starting bids. Being under the minimum bid will mean you won't receive any impressions from that keyword, but keep your bids as low as possible (this is also an art, that is how to place bids on keywords). Anyway, I wouldn't suggest using anything over $1 bids, since those are high competition keywords, where there are big

players and, as an indie author, it is something we want to avoid going up against
- Use negative keywords (Negative Exact) if needed. If you try a keyword term in the Amazon search bar and it lists several other products, not just books, you can use these product categories as negative terms (like "bags", "DVD" etc.). This will help to reduce costs and improve targeting

You pay fees after clicks, not impressions on Amazon Ads. This is slightly misunderstood by many marketeers, so they want to stuff as many keywords into the campaign as they can. It certainly has the effect that the book's ad receives tons of impressions. But on the other side, 90% of keywords won't convert and there could be a lot of false clicks when the visitor quickly realizes the book has nothing to do with his or her search query.

Now you have to enter your credit card info. Amazon will charge your card after you reach the credit limit (it starts at $50 than later it will increase to $150, $200, etc.).

After doing all this you may start your first campaign, which will be in review status at first. Amazon's representatives review all campaigns. They don't accept book genres like erotic romances, drug or medication-related books, financial products like cryptocurrencies, and other categories. You need to ensure that your book isn't in these categories. They are checking to be sure certain standards are met. For example, you need to use English keywords in an Amazon.com campaign, and German language keywords in an Amazon.de campaign.

Now here are some common mistakes you want to avoid.

Keyword cannibalization (one of my favourite terms)

This is the case when you use the same keyword phrases in two of your campaigns. This basically means that you bid over your own bid. I have seen this several times where the campaign editor uses the same keywords in multiple campaigns with different bids. It means their keyword would only be used in one campaign, where it is listed as the highest bid. Keep track of your keywords that appear in a campaign.

Using high competition keywords

If you need to pay over $1.00 for one click then it is a high competition keyword. Try to avoid using them; they could destroy your ACoS (Advertising Cost of Sale). This is why I prefer ultra-relevant keywords, which have lower bids and a higher chance that the visitor will buy your book.

Advertising a book without reviews

Four out of ten authors think that with Amazon Ads he or she can get a lot of reviews. That is not true. If you start advertising a completely new book without any reviews, your conversion rate will be close to zero. On Amazon, people check the reviews, and any books without reviews are suspicious. No matter how good the description or the title is.

Always wait for 5-10 reviews before starting any paid ads on Amazon.

Using generic keywords

"YA fantasy" is a terrible keyword: up 10,000 authors and publishers are competing for this exact keyword. It is considered too generic to bring relevant results to your new campaign. In the case of these keywords, the ACoS is usually above 100%, which will never bring you positive ROI. Also, these generic keywords are too expensive to bid; they are usually above $1.50. In the case of Amazon Ads, we try to use specific keywords as we can. Just to stick to our example "YA medieval fantasy books" would work better as a keyword.

DAY 16

Using too many keywords

I saw campaigns with up to 300 keywords. None of them were effective. Why? They used a lot of irrelevant keywords that aren't connected to the book's topic and it is almost impossible to evaluate and review the keywords' performance bi-weekly. The promoters usually let the ad run for 4-5 months when they realize they have still low sales, but Amazon charges a lot of cash for Ads. This part is painful. This is why we say there are usually 30-40 relevant keywords to your book and overall you don't need more than 50 keywords for your campaign.

People don't adjust bids and evaluate keywords

As mentioned above you need to check your campaign bi-weekly. This means you need to pause keywords which don't deliver sales. We expect one sale out of 8-12 clicks, but if a keyword is above 30 clicks without sales it won't be effective in the future. Pause them. Adjusting bids mean, you slightly raise or lower the bid for an exact keyword. There could be a seasonal fluctuation, for example before the holiday season bids are skyrocketing. Bids could rise in November from $0.85 to $1.20 and then drop to $0.85 in February.

DAY 17

FACEBOOK GROUPS FOLLOW UP

This is the follow-up day to check back in on all those Facebook Groups. You probably joined several groups where relevant people (potential readers) are discussing books. Joining in the conversation is the best way to get some attention within the group. If you don't do this first and "cold-post" your book, it will seem pushy. The worst thing that can happen is you get an instant ban from the group and your post is then removed immediately. So we should be careful.

What and how to go about posting in these groups?

- **A gentle, personal message**: you just wrote a "romance", which is about "a poor little girl" who wants to find "a happy life in the big city."
- You don't need to have your own "book post" in the group. **Mention it by joining a conversation (comment)** of another relevant post. Remember the first comment of the post receives almost as much attention as the post itself. This is why a lot of pages put links in their first comment.
- **Ask!** Ask the crowd's opinion about your book's topic or story: People love to answer questions because they love to express their opinion and

DAY 17

this is what we need. The more they look up your book, the better for you.
- **You don't need to add the book sales link**: Put only your title in a post or comment, so people won't have the feeling you are pushy, and trust me if you get this right they will Google your title and find the Amazon link.

What To Avoid

- Never post your book's Amazon link without any comment beneath it! It is called "spamming" and will only ruin your book's reputation
- If you share your book **use your own creative description**, not the one Amazon automatically generates when inserting the link. Facebook prefers visual (image, video) posts, so the post will receive more impressions by group members

Now you can do the posting or commenting. Please remind yourself no matter how gently you want to just share it will always be a pushy move and you might find it uncomfortable. Promoting a book is like promoting a business of yours, where you will receive money as a result.

DAY 18

INFLUENCERS FOLLOW UP

You will probably have received several messages back from influencers by now. Try to answer them on the fly (this can be a little tiresome). Prepare your requirements ahead of time to make this go more smoothly, and don't use the terms:

- What will it cost you? (some influencers don't have a flat rate, so you have to offer a certain amount like $20, plus a free copy of your book)
- Where he or she will post the review (Amazon, Goodreads, Instagram, on a website or any of these in combination)

Once you agree on the terms, you will need to get an address and you need to notify them of when he or she will receive the paperback copy if he or she doesn't request an electronic copy (some Influencers prefer Amazon Kindle).

In both cases, it is likely that you will have to send the "reading fee" prior to receiving the review, in most cases using Paypal. It is always a risk. This is why you should avoid as much risk as you can. Never send $100 to an amateur influencer, and don't forget that the number of followers they have is not everything!

DAY 19

Track your Influencer discussions in an excel file, so you will always know the status of the process. Once the review is out, save the link and track reactions. Usually, the majority of traffic from influencers will come in the first 3 days. These reviews will be a reference for your book and create value. You can always quote them and use them later on.

Based on my experiences it is better to negotiate with multiple small influencers than one "big one."

DAY 19

GOODREADS SELF-SERVE ADVERTISING

In the last five years of utilizing this advertising platform, I discovered some basic flaws in it. Whilst it does offer good targeting, you can't target certain specific niches.

Since the whole website is about researching your next read, the ad placement doesn't feel natural and you won't catch the plus one book ad next to 10-15 books on the side panel. In a noisy environment like this, there should be an option to highlight an ad (this is done much better on Amazon).

Don't misunderstand me. Goodreads is one of my favourite websites, but this form of advertising simply isn't worth it. Maybe Goodreads has also noticed this and they will rework the complete self-serve ad platform, as the current form won't be available from February 2020.

I will cover "Goodreads Giveaways" later on.

GENERAL COMMENT

Now, this is a fairly new or unknown platform, but it is worth learning to create ads here.

Please note that not every book genre is ideal for every platform. Different websites have different audiences. Let's see what genres fit in the best on different platforms:

- Quora Advertising – Primarily for nonfiction genres (Technology, Society)
- Pinterest Ads – Primarily good for fiction (Romance, Cookbooks) – Majority of users are Female
- Reddit Ads – Primarily good for fiction books (Thrillers, Fantasy, Sci-fi) – it has a balanced user base, but the specific demographic of the community depends on the subreddit in question

DAY 19

If you are planning to use one of the above platforms then keep in mind **you want to find the exact niche community** who will be interested in your topic. If you plan to run a general, wide campaign just because the site has many visitors, you will only waste money.

QUORA ADS

Since either Quora, Pinterest, or Reddit isn't Facebook or Instagram, the ad competition is lower, which means you may get cheaper clicks on average as opposed to the more popular platforms (Google or Facebook Ads).

Always try to target desktop visitors on these platforms. On mobile we don't "surf," and we don't open random windows. On a desktop, we are willing to give new things a try. Also, it is important to realize that the majority of online sales are happening on a desktop. **Desktop has 2x-2.5x higher conversion rates** than mobile. It is a huge difference now but will disappear by 2025.

The basic process of setting up a Quora Ad is straightforward.

When it comes to Quora Ads, my favorite targeting method is "Contextual Targeting" > "Questions," Take your time and find 10-15 relevant questions connecting to your topic.

If you wrote a book about Python programming, then "Which is the best book for learning python for absolute beginners on their own?" is exactly one where you want to show your book to the audience.

I really love Quora, because a lot of people are thinking in questions, and we ask questions naturally to find a solution to our problems, even if it is entertainment, such as "What are the best books …?", "Where to start …?" etc. So the key here is to hyper-target your audience, using questions they are likely to ask.

You may use the marketing creative we prepared at the beginning and try to answer the question in one line to make visitors click your book.

Start your campaign.

DAY 20

PINTEREST ADS

Though I prefer visual creatives, sometimes it is good to put text on an image next to your book. But, on Pinterest that just isn't the case! Unless you wrote a book that is full of memes!

DAY 20

With Pinterest Ads, you have to have the perfect creative for your book. Perhaps take a copy out into nature and shoot some photos of it. Then adjust it in Photoshop. You have to have a colourful photo with no opacity and no grey spots.

Once you have the right photo, set up the campaign ("Promoted Pins"), target your audience, and enter your landing page. Some tips during the setup:

- Handle your picture like a fashion item; choose simple, light background colors that compliment your book
- Your keyword list is just as important here
- Pay after clicks
- Run an ad before the holiday season (Christmas); you will be able to sell 3 times more books in December than in any other month of the year
- Use the right aspect ratio (600 x 900 pixels is optimal)

You will be impressed by how many impressions a Pinterest ad could generate for your book!

DAY 21

GENERAL COMMENT - REST DAY

Have you ever wondered if you should be writing more books? Several years ago, I met with an author, and I asked him what kind of marketing activity he did.

He said, *"I write another book."*

He didn't really care about marketing; he wrote fantasy books, a long series that consisted of 5-7 titles as far as I can remember. He had a point.

Having multiple books is good marketing in itself.

People don't just buy books. They check the author, and if they make a positive impression, they will be more likely to buy his or her next work.

So instead of one book, have three or four!

DAY 22

AMAZON ADS BID REVIEW

Check your Amazon Sponsored Product campaign, created on Day 16. You now need to handle and adjust keyword bids. The Amazon Ads Platform has an

DAY 22

automatic bid offering function called "Suggested bid." It suggests the median (the most typical) bid for a specific keyword.

You will want to adjust bids to:

- Be in the range (shown under "Suggested bid"). If your bid is out of the range, it won't receive any impressions.
- If the keyword is ultra-relevant, use a higher bid than the median so you will receive more impressions.
- If the keyword is generic or less-relevant, use lower bids, and try to keep these keywords in the budget.
- There are keywords that are also used for non-book products (pills, nutrition, electronics). These are high competition keywords and usually, the median is over $1. Try to keep your bids under $1 and even consider stopping bidding entirely if they go over this amount. An alternative could be that you enter "book" or "books" after the keyword, creating an entirely new keyword. This method will narrow the search term and hopefully will be available at a lower bid price.

The range of bids is constantly changing, based on the **popularity** of the keyword. There are global seasons when keyword bids are cheaper like in March or June and there are months when there is huge competition between book-related keywords like November, before Christmas.

ACoS (Advertising Cost of Sale) is a metric that could help us when deciding about bids. Hence, ACoS isn't the best metric since it doesn't deal with your revenue share. This is something you should do manually:

Net revenue = Sales revenue of campaign – Campaign cost (Sales revenue of Campaign = Sales * Revenue share after one purchase)

If you don't like math, you may still use ACoS as an indicator, since it will be always in front of you:

- >25% ACoS – Ineffective keywords
- 15-25% ACoS – Good keywords
- 5-15% ACoS – Effective keywords
- <5% ACoS – Ultra effective keywords

If a keyword has an ACoS under 15%, then it is an effective and working keyword; if it is even under 5% then it is an excellent keyword. Keywords between 15% and 25% are good keywords and still worthwhile to use in the long term.

DAY 22

Keywords over 25%-30% are keywords that should make you stop and evaluate; never keep them in the long-term keyword mix just because you will have "one plus" keywords to use. If a keyword has a 35% ACoS but you want to "push your book," keep them in for a certain period only (1-2 months).

A common mistake is that people are evaluating ACoS after only 1-2 weeks. This is the time when we see 100-200% ACoS keywords or keywords with no sales, just spent money. Remember ACoS is a statistical metric. After 1-2 weeks there won't be enough data to provide you any significant statistics. Also, for this same reason, ignore ACoS if your total spending is less than $50.

In Amazon Ads, you are paying for clicks, not impressions. This means when somebody clicks on your ad, he or she needs to receive exactly what they expected based on the keyword they entered. So, be straightforward with the title, subtitle, and the book description.

DAY 23

EMAIL MARKETING

On your website, you have the chance to collect visitors' email addresses by gently asking them if they are interested in news or future releases, and having them enter their email address to receive these. An email address is of value in itself, and email marketing is still a viable marketing concept in 2020.

Mailchimp, Sendgrid, and AWeber are good email marketing services. If you want to use them for one book then it is most likely they would also be free, albeit with certain limitations.These are services are easily integrated into your WordPress site with plugins. This way, any of your visitors can subscribe to your mailing list by entering their name and email. This way you can manage your subscribers and track them.

Emails

Never send emails without a reason or without permission.

Typical reasons which may interest your subscribers:

- Important event connected to the book or author

- The book is on "sale" or "free" for a limited time
- Next book from the author will be available on this date

Emails still have a good conversion rate and generate good traffic for the landing page. If you have time, create a landing page for your email and redirect traffic there, not just to the main page of your website.

Never stuff too many links into your email (one bold link is ideal), or readers may miss the topic and then become random traffic on your website.

There are a lot of good looking email design templates, but my experience is that an honest personal note is just as effective as an ultra-decorative HTML email. Create a personal email using your domain and send out the emails from this address, like authorsname@mydomain.com. This will implicate you wrote a personal message, which will have a better response rate.

At the end of the day, email marketing is still a big player in 2020; you can even purchase email lists if you want on the web, though this is a kind of grey area since the emergence of GDPR.

DAY 24

BOOK AWARDS

Maybe by now you have found a lot of websites where you can enter your book to win a book award.

We have to be clear about these awards and realistic about our expectations. It is a big business but mainly for the award organizers. Of course there is a prize pool (which is only a fraction of the fees that they collect when you enter). So, are these awards objective? Never.

So why is it worth it to enter?

Only if you want **a badge** of "Award Winning Book." It looks really good on the front cover of your book, but realistically, there is limited marketing value. One thing is for sure, it won't change your life, and neither will it drastically change your book's sales numbers.

How should I decide on which award to enter?

- Don't bother yourself with "cover awards" or "best book of the month" awards.
- Never participate in awards where individuals can vote on books.
- Don't pay pots of money just to enter a book award! (Keep your costs under $100).

DAY 24

- Search for indie book awards; you don't want to compete with big publishing houses.
- There are several book awards where there is a nomination phase (You receive a badge of honor, but maybe you won't receive any prize at all), remember you only need the badge, so these awards are better for you.
- Only participate in one or two awards! (Keep an eye on your budget).

It often takes several months until the award is decided, so don't have any expectations about winning; if it happens (sometimes it will) then it means your cover and your book are really good (in the top 1%).

To give you some further help, here are some reliable Awards & Contests:

- Adventure Writers Competition - Clive Cussler Collector's Society
- Arnold Bennett Prize - Arnold Bennett Society
- B.R.A.G. Medallion - indieBRAG, LLC
- Big Five Competition - Words With Jam
- Book of the Year Awards (IAN) - Independent Author Network
- BookLife - Publishers Weekly
- EPIC's eBook Awards - Electronic Publishing Industry Coalition

- GCLS Literary Awards (The Goldies) - Golden Crown Literary Society
- Goodreads Choice Awards – Goodreads
- James River Writers - James River Writers
- Kindle Book Awards - Kindle Book Review
- North Street Book Prize- Winning Writers
- SPR Awards - Self Publishing Review
- Tom Howard/Margaret Reid Poetry Contest - Winning Writers
- Writer Advice Scintillating Starts Contest - Writer Advice

DAY 25

AMAZON PAGE

I know maybe the following checklist is self-evident for a lot of authors who are using KDP or any self-publishing platform, but I rarely see perfect indie book pages. So, it will benefit you hugely just to spend one day to review, correct, or complete your book's page.

Let's take a look at the typical shortcomings:

- The different versions of the book aren't linked properly (Kindle, Paperback, Hardcover, or Audible) - All you need to do is write a

message to the support team and they will link the different versions, though this mistake is rare since CreateSpace and KDP merged into one platform
- The book's categories are not visible under "Amazon Best Sellers Rank." It seems your book has no categories – A lot of people don't know that in Amazon Author Central "Help" section there is a "Contact Us" form with which you can add more categories by clicking "Update Information About a Book" and selecting "Browse Categories" at the end of which you can enter your desired category via email or phone
- There are no Editorial Reviews on your book's Amazon page – This is also an option which is available on Amazon Author Central, if you go to the "Books" page in the "Editorial Reviews" tab you can directly enter the desired reviews of your book
- There is no author picture – This is something you can also add through Amazon Author Central, just be sure the image style matches your book
- Use HTML in your book's description – You can add bold text, italic, and even list elements in your description

DAY 26

SOCIAL MEDIA AND SIGNITURE

A lot of people think marketing is hard and are not aware of the easier techniques.

It is likely that you wrote your book as a hobby and that's OK. What most writers don't realize is that having a book (even if it is self-published) means you deserve an "**Author**" signature.

Go to your email client and create one. No need to add your book title, just an author website or social pages. You may use this signature when you are sending emails to non-professionals. Maybe you don't realize, but having an author signature at the end of your emails will generate a lot of leads.

LinkedIn is for professional networking, but it is also a great place to **publicize your book**. If you update your page, a big chunk of your network will instantly get notified about your new work, even if it is a hobby. Trust me, it will be a really popular ice breaker question in conversation *"Hey, I saw you wrote a book! What is it about?"*. And yes, people do buy books written by a business associate (just for fun).

DAY 27

Don't forget about your other social media profiles, Twitter, Facebook, and Instagram are also good places to update your identity. One other place is Quora, but we will speak about this more later.

If you have time you can also update cover images, put a photo out about the book, all of this is to try to get the visitors to ask "What is this book? Why is it on your page?"

DAY 27

INSTAGRAM

The 27th day of your book is always special, think of it as something unique that people do not see everyday. Today's marketing is the content itself, including the author.

A lot of readers are interested about the author, because he or she is also part of the story. Just think about it, if you read something interesting wouldn't you also be interested in who wrote it?

Today (in case you don't have a better idea) **post behind the scenes pictures** to Instagram. Did I forget to mention that this is the primary social media in 2020? Well it is.

DAY 28

Facebook and even Twitter are secondary (unless you have built up a significant audience on these platforms).

Back to the task at hand. Do you have a special place that inspires you? Take a pic. Do you have a favourite place to write? Take a pic. Do you find it too plain? Focus your phone (camera) on the interesting part! It is all about the details! Your favourite childhood game, your lucky pen, just show it to the crowd. They will appreciate your honesty, that you want to show part of your life to them. And don't forget to tell the story: why is that particular object, or place, important to you!?

DAY 28

GENERAL COMMENT - REST DAY

If you follow the steps recommended in this book, please don't forget: nobody has followed this exact process yet. Maybe you are the first one, but even after just reading these marketing ideas your head should be full of garbage (or not?) at this point. In the next two days, I want to draw your focus back to the important things. If you read just the next two days' stuff you will more for your book than 80% of authors.

Keep your marketing list clean and tidy.

DAY 29

INFLUENCERS FOLLOW UP

I know, I know, no more Influencers! They won't help, they don't want to even answer. **Remember, we need those influencers!**

First thing: let's clean our excel tracking sheet (or any notes you created). There are two types of people among influencers:

- Category 1: They have the intention of doing the review and posting it, but they need regular follow up to remind them
- Category 2: They have no intention of reviewing your book and you simply can't seal the deal

Decide whether any of your ongoing negotiations are in Category 1 or Category 2.

In the case of category 1, send out a reminder email or message. It takes only 5 minutes but may result in closing the deal. Most people feel motivated only if they are pushed; in other cases, they may simply forget about the task, even if they want to do the review. In this case, just be a **gentle project manager**.

If they're in category 2, just cross the influencer off your list and let it go. You can quickly identify them by problematic negotiation:

- You can't agree on the price.
- He or she doesn't want to send his or her address to you.
- You can't agree where to post the review.

Accept the fact that only half of the "I want to review your book" comments will end up in real reviews. It's not about you or about the influencer, it's just the way the world works.

Finish cleaning up your spreadsheet before pitching to any new influencers!

DAY 30

AMAZON ADVERTISING

As said, on Day 28 we have a lot of shit (it's not just Scalzi who uses vulgar language) going on. Let's review the most important points from the last 30 days:

Reviews on Amazon and Goodreads
Importance 5/5

DAY 30

If you have less than five on Amazon and less than ten on Goodreads, drop your principles and go to your best friend and do a review together. I know a lot of people who would never buy a book without any reviews. A lot of people say that real books start selling at 100 reviews (which isn't true, by the way). But these are false beliefs and you won't be able to fix these anytime soon.

So let's swallow the bitter pill and collect the first twenty reviews, no matter what.

Amazon Advertising Sponsored Ads
Importance 3/5

The best part of Amazon Ads is that your book and the visitors are already on the same website. This is a strong advantage. On the other hand, as described earlier, we experience that Amazon Ads are becoming less effective in the last months, which could result in many negative ROI campaigns. If you want this form of advertising, use only ultra-relevant keywords.

Listopia lists
Importance 4/5

Don't be lazy; do the things that cost you no money but do take time. List your book on Librarything, find relevant Listopia lists on Goodreads, post your book on Riffle, Listal, and any other sites.

DAY 30

Creating a marketing creative (Image)
Importance 4/5

If anybody searches for your book on Google, they will see two things:

1. Your book's cover
2. Your marketing creative

The majority of them are able to decide whether this book is worth another click or not based only on these two factors. This is why I emphasize the importance of your cover; it can have huge marketing value if done right.

Whenever you want to share your book, you will most probably want to share this image:

- If you send a picture along with an interview to an online magazine
- If you want to re-share your book on social media
- If you want to put your book into a profile

There are practically unlimited opportunities to use your visual marketing tool.

THE SECOND MONTH
DAY 31-62

DAY 31-38

KINDLE COUNTDOWN DEALS (KCD)

Now, this marketing method is something that is really useful for indie authors. It wasn't the situation some years ago. But finally, Countdown Deals received a dedicated place on Amazon: Kindle Store > Kindle Countdown Deals, and yes people are looking for deals. This is an extra place where your book will be listed for a limited time. Also, if your book is enrolled in KDP Select and you earn 70% royalty after Kindle sales, this percentage will remain, even if your book discount price is at $0.99 (your royalty rate would then be $0.69).

A Countdown Deal usually lasts 5 to 7 days, with 7 being the maximum. One criterion is that your book should be in KDP Select for more than 30 days.

Let the world (or at least the US and UK where this promotional option is available) know your dates! Publish the Countdown Deal's dates on your social media. Don't be afraid! This is finally a good use case for your website and social media sites.

It is an important question considering whether or not you need to do a "big" promotion for Countdown Deals because remember lowering the price of your book can have a big impact on your bottom line. For example, Bookbub has a really pricey promotional package for Countdown Deals. I don't think it is worth it. For we indie authors balancing costs and returns will always be important. Use your own channels whenever possible!

FREE BOOK PROMOTION (FBP)

This is the little brother of Countdown Deals.

Choose either-or!

If you have a cheap book, this could be the solution. Don't be afraid that everybody will suddenly download your book for free and no one will ever pay for it. This is simply not how it works.

In both cases (KCD or FBP) your book's Amazon Best Sellers Rank will improve, thanks to the additional downloads. It will help your book to **rank higher in overall Amazon search results**, which is a healthy way to improve your sales in the long term.

This is the reason why both KCD and FBP could be a good solution for you. The worst thing that can happen is that your sales numbers won't be any higher, but your risk is minimal; remember the more people read your book (even for free) the more likely your audience is to get broader.

DAY 39-46

QUORA

Finally, one of my favourites, and a mainly unknown method I want to share with you. It is free and fun.

I already wrote about Quora Advertising, which is a decent way to spend some money on marketing, but what if I told you there is an even better (free) solution?

Quora is a question-answering platform, where people are coming to find answers. Since the launch of Quora (2009) almost 38 million questions have been answered. That is a big number and trust me there are a lot of questions that are related to your book's topic:

- Product related questions – usually good for fiction books ("Which is the best romance book in Hindi?")

- Topic related questions, when the reader would find the answer in your book – usually good for non-fiction books ("How do I prepare for a data scientist interview?")
- Open questions where they are looking to receive some recommendations – good for both fiction and non-fiction ("What are some books that expand our mind?")

Now it is time to research and choose some questions that are related to your book.

Answer them (if you are new to the platform, don't use ANY links, so you may avoid banning your account). Be fresh and honest in your answers- avoid any marketing bullshit! If you recommend, recommend other products, too. Don't be selfish and let the reader choose.

As you may have noticed there is a "**credentials**" headline next to your name above the answer and this is your private place where you can add your book's title like "**Author of marketing book XY**". This is where the magic happens. Do you remember when I said that people are often interested more about authors than books? They will click on your profile, and check out who you are! **This is where you can post some of your books with links**.

The more questions you answer, the more profile visits you will have! This method even works when you "just" answer a random question. It may happen that visitors get randomly interested in you and this will end up in sales. Quora is an excellent marketing place for writers.

But be cautious! Answering questions is addictive! Keep in mind you have limited time for writing, and while you are answering a question you aren't working on your next book.

Anyway, helping people is always a good thing. Answer Quora questions regularly, and try to find questions which receive a little bit more attention (followed by more people).

DAY 47-54

REDDIT

I was never good with Reddit, and if you aren't using the platform on a daily basis, you may follow my recommendations.

Why is it worth it?

DAY 47-54

A Reddit comment is like a sticky post. It will be available for Google later on, unlike Facebook posts, which are harder to recover.

Some years ago, one of my friends told me that he tried posting on Reddit in a relevant non-fiction topic, and his book only received criticism and abuse. But on that day he had more sales than in the last month combined.

Reddit hates advertising and this is something I can understand. This is why you need to be as gentle as possible with any posts.

What you will need?

- Aged account, with a lot of karma
- An excellent, well-thought-out text post that raises questions in readers and hopefully generates interest in your book (If you just drop in "I just published a book in a topic this and this") you will receive an instant **shadow ban**

What does shadow banning mean?

It is a tricky way to ban your account from the entire Reddit platform. From your perspective (login with your account) nothing changes, but nobody will see your posts and comments, except you. You may request to remove the ban from subreddit admin, but it isn't likely they will do that.

So back to our topic:

What I will need?

Professional help- go visit marketing forums for Reddit professionals who have multiple high karma reddit accounts. They will know how to approach your topic and book. They will most likely charge you somewhere between $50-$100. Don't forget to ask for upvotes if possible, since it isn't enough to write something out, as only upvoted topics get attention. Also, find the best places where you (or the professional) can share your story. Don't choose subreddits with very few members, ideal subreddits are somewhere between 5,000-100,000 members.

If you are doing everything right, your sales will get a sudden boost (you will sell 10-100 copies). There are also free to try out opportunities, such as r/books, subreddit's "New Releases" weekly thread.

So prepare your stomach for some rude comments and perhaps ask them to be gentle at least.

DAY 55-62

TIKTOK

Are you writing for younger generations?

Recording a 15/60 sec video on TikTok could be both fun and effective as marketing. The platform went viral this year and 41% of its users are aged between 16 and 24.

There is only one problem, TikTok's short videos aren't even close in style to Youtube videos. These short videos need to be fun and trendy. If you would like to create videos for TikTok it could be useful to talk to a teenager.

We are keeping our eyes on this platform because at the moment there are no ads on the platform. You couldn't redirect visitors only to your Instagram page. In terms of marketing, it is similar to Instagram, but it has many restrictions.

AMAZON ADS FOLLOW UP

Time to review our ongoing campaigns, sales, and costs.

The basic metric is ROI (Return on Investment). For us return is the royalty rate which is the result of sales. Let's see some common scenarios:

1. Sum of the sales is still lower than the campaign's cost (Worst case scenario)

2. Sum of the royalties coming from sales is lower than the campaign's cost (still a bad case scenario)
3. Sum of the royalties is higher than the campaign's cost (Best case scenario)

Worst and bad case scenarios

If a campaign costs more than the royalties you earn, it could mean several things:

- You have an unprofessional cover which isn't converting (as mentioned on Day -120)
- Your blurb isn't specific or doesn't make the book attractive to the reader
- Your book has no reviews (or very few); in some cases, there are only bad reviews
- Your ad campaign uses irrelevant keywords and you receive random clicks only

What to do?

First check whether there are any keywords that have under <15% ACoS, if this is the case then you can cross the first two lines off the above list.

If you haven't got any keywords with good ACoS value, evaluate what else could be the problem! Ask an objective friend to take a quick peek at your book's Amazon page and your cover. Ask for his or her honest opinion. Sometimes it takes only 2 minutes to find out what the problem is.

Fix it. Maybe it will take several days, but it is worth it. A book is a living thing, it changes constantly (receives revisions, new editions, new covers, sometimes translations).

Best case scenario

Remember there is always room for improvement. Try to add more keywords to your mix. It will be surprisingly easy at the beginning, after the initial setup.

You could still find keywords that don't work and pause them. No worries though, there are a lot of keywords out there.

Consider keeping working campaigns running for the long term. If a campaign delivers sales, there is no reason to stop it.

THE THIRD MONTH AND BEYOND
DAY 63-100

DAY 63-70

GOODREADS GIVEAWAY

It isn't the biggest shot in indie book marketing, since it costs a flat fee to start a Goodreads Giveaway (Starting at $119). Several years ago, it was free. The budget seems to be the following:

- Entry fee $119 ($599 premium) for Goodreads
- Cost of paperback copies e.g. 10 x $5
- Cost of international delivery 10 x $10 (or you may geo restrict the audience)

A Goodreads Giveaway starts at $270 (plus your time) and you will most probably receive 1,500-5,000 entries and another 15,000-25,000 impressions.

Also, a giveaway is a long project as it is listed for 15-30 days on Goodreads, where you receive the majority of entries at the beginning and then in the last 1-2 days. Another problem is that a lot of people are just hoping to get lucky. If they don't win, they won't buy your book from Amazon, even if it seems they are interested.

In the basic package, you receive only the winner's data, and you won't have any access to the other people who didn't win. It is a big loss, so perhaps don't approach them in case of another deal.

Overall, I don't recommend a Goodreads Giveaway just for generating sales, but it is a fun way to rule the market if you already have a (fairly) good selling book; in this case, the entry fee would be a reasonable cost.

DAY 71-78

INTERNATIONAL BOOK FAIRS

International Book Fairs are more like an expo of books. You will see more books than you ever imagined. The season starts in March and ends in December.

First, let's see the list of the year more or less ordered in date:

- **New Delhi World Book Fair - New Delhi, India**
- Books for Children, Young Adults, and Parents - Poznań, Poland
- Emirates Airline Festival of Literature - Dubai, United Arab Emirates
- Moscow International Book Fair - Moscow, Russia

- Buchmesse im Ried - Stockstadt am Rhein, Germany
- Bursa Book Fair - Bursa, Turkey
- **The London Book Fair - London, U.K.**
- LivreParis - Paris, France
- Leipzig Book Fair - Leipzig, Germany
- Alexandria International Book Fair - Alexandria, Egypt
- Kuala Lumpur International Book Fair - Kuala Lumpur, Malaysia
- Bologna Children's Book Fair - Bologna, Italy
- Izmir Book Fair - Izmir, Turkey
- Prague International Book Fair - Prague, Czech Republic
- Québec International Book Fair - Québec, Canada
- Boekenfestijn Book Festival - Kortrijk, Belgium
- Eurasian International Book Fair, Astana - Astana, Kazakhstan
- **Abu Dhabi International Book Fair - Abu Dhabi, UAE**
- Tehran International Book Fair - Tehran, Iran
- Budapest International Book Festival - Budapest, Hungary
- Bogota International Book Fair - Bogota, Colombia

- Buenos Aires Book Fair - Buenos Aires, Argentina
- Geneva Book Fair - Geneva, Switzerland
- Berlin Art Book Festival - Berlin, Germany
- Nigeria International Book Fair - Lagos, Nigeria
- Thessaloniki Book Fair – Greece
- **Turin International Book Fair - Turin, Italy**
- WBF Warsaw Book Fair - Warsaw, Poland
- Kingsmead College Book Fair - Johannesburg, South Africa
- **BookExpo America - New York City, USA**
- Bookfest International Book Fair - Bucharest, Romania
- Lisbon Book Fair - Lisbon, Portugal
- International Book Fair for Small Publishers and Private Presses - Mayence, Germany
- Tbilisi International Book Fair - Tbilisi, Georgia
- Madrid Book Fair - Madrid, Spain
- Firsts – London's Rare Book Fair - London, UK
- Seoul International Book Fair - Seoul, South Korea
- BookFest Malaysia - Kuala Lumpur, Malaysia
- Melbourne Rare Book Fair - Melbourne, Australia
- **Hong Kong Book Fair - Hong Kong**
- International Book Fair of Lima - Lima, Peru
- Toronto Art Book Fair - Toronto, Canada

DAY 71-78

- Cologne Art Book Fair - Cologne, Germany
- Nepal International Book Fair - Kathmandu, Nepal
- Beijing International Book Fair - Beijing, China
- Ghana International Book Fair - Accra, Ghana
- Rio de Janeiro International Book Fair - Rio de Janeiro, Brazil
- Library of Congress National Book Festival - Washington D.C., USA
- Jozi Book Fair - Johannesburg, South Africa
- Baku Book Fair - Baku, Azerbaijan
- Latvian Book Fair - Riga, Latvia
- Indonesia International Book Fair – Indonesia
- South African Book Fair - Johannesburg, South Africa
- Manila International Book Fair - Pasay, Philippines
- Göteborg Book Fair - Gothenburg, Sweden
- Amman International Book Fair - Amman, Jordan
- Nairobi International Book Fair - Nairobi, Kenya
- **Tokyo International Book Fair - Tokyo, Japan**
- Zimbabwe International Book Fair - Harare, Zimbabwe
- **Frankfurt Book Fair - Frankfurt, Germany**
- Krakow International Book Fair - Krakow, Poland

- Helsinki Book Fair - Helsinki, Finland
- Antwerp Book Fair - Antwerp, Belgium
- Santiago Book Fair - Santiago, Chile
- LIBER International Book Fair - Barcelona or Madrid, Spain
- International Belgrade Book Fair - Belgrade, Serbia
- Art Book Fair Berlin - Berlin, Germany
- Editions Artists Book Fair - New York, USA
- Vienna International Book Fair - Vienna, Austria
- Riyadh International Book Fair - Riyadh, KSA
- Shanghai International Children's Book Fair - Shanghai, China
- Salon du livre de Montréal - Montréal, Canada
- Slovenian Book Fair - Ljubljana, Slovenia
- **FIL de Guadalajara - Guadalajara, Mexico**
- Sharjah International Book Fair - Sharjah, UAE
- Malta Book Festival - Valletta, Malta
- Bibliotéka Bratislava - Bratislava, Slovakia
- International Children and Young Adults Book Fair (FILIJ) - Mexico City, Mexico
- Istanbul Book Fair - Istanbul, Turkey
- Dublin Book Festival - Dublin, Ireland
- Pula Festival of Books and Authors - Pula, Croatia
- Moscow Non/Fiction Book Fair - Moscow, Russia

- Rome Book Fair - Rome, Italy
- Sofia International Book Fair - Sofia, Bulgaria
- Jeddah International Book Fair - Jeddah, Saudi Arabia
- Karachi International Book Fair - Karachi, Pakistan

I also highlighted the most influential ones.

Lookup the closest location to you and search for dates. Book fairs are only valuable if you are present, physically. It is also a great experience, as you will learn a lot as an author on these expos. Several book fairs have some specialties like sticking to one genre such as showcasing only YA books (young adult).

You may wonder what if I would put my own new book on the stand?

There are a lot of opportunities and online service providers who are willing to do this. You pay out $200-$500 to them, you send several copies of your book, and boom, done! The effectiveness of this is most likely minimal.

Ok, so what book fairs are good for?

At book fairs, you will be able to speak with people, and it is a good opportunity to network.

- The most important publishers in that region will be present at book fairs; don't go with your manuscript (but you may store some paperback copies in your bag), but if you do a professional first touch, they may be more likely to take a peek at your manuscript later on
- Exchange your contacts, prepare a professional business card (50 should be enough)
- But most importantly you will find **a lot of new ideas** about books (covers, the attitude of publishers, etc.), **take photo notes**
- If you are going with a friend, take a photo of you holding your book at the event. Cheat a little bit!
- Contact foreign publishing houses. As a self-published author, you will have limited resources to translate and publish books to other languages, but it is an important way to grow your audience

What I learned about these events is that these are primarily for publishing houses, not for authors or readers. Of course, as an avid reader, it is like heaven, but there is too much noise. Approximately 100,000 to 500,000 books are present at these events. Break up with the idea of marketing your book at a book fair and try to focus on getting in touch with publishers, this should be the ultimate goal of being present at a book fair.

DAY 79-86

SEND YOUR BOOK FOR FREE IF REQUESTED

I heard this story from one of close my friends after he wrote his nonfiction book and made the book available on Amazon and in paperback and Kindle forms. He literally noted visitors on his website, that if you send him a personal request, he will send you a full copy of his book for free.

First, I thought it made no sense. You are giving away (ok, just PDF copies but it is almost the same) electronic copies to those who are already interested in your book and would buy it anyway.

He said *"no, they don't want to buy my book, they want to read it... It is a gesture on my side, to let readers first read, then decide whether to buy or not"*.

The thing is, this story becomes interesting when I first read about the success story of Paulo Coelho, the Brazilian author who published The Alchemist in 1988. The first English edition was released in 1993 by HarperCollins which helped him to achieve his breakthrough. However, only a few people know that he was willing to give away his book for free. If you search for the article "Alchemist Author Pirates His Own Books" then you will see that Coelho said almost the same thing *"I went to BitTorrent and I got all my pirate editions...And I created a site called The Pirate Coelho...I thought that this is fantastic. You give to the reader the possibility of reading your books and choosing whether to buy it or not."*

From a marketing point of view, this mentality is the future and both my friend and Coelho predicted it. As they say, *"a good product sells itself,"* but first people need to have a taste!

Just to give you some more insight, my friend already sent out more than 200 copies (not a big number anyway) vie email to readers, and received a bunch of Goodreads reviews in exchange. He already received something back! Of course, he isn't able to estimate how many books were sold thanks to this "gesture" but giving away books doesn't kill the business. It generates discussion, a personal touch with the author and this is all we need since everyone is an influencer in a sense.

DAY 87-94

GENERAL COMMENT

Well, life won't stop at day 100, but if you managed to arrive at this point and you have already completed the steps outlined in this book, you are a good way along the road to becoming a full-time author (or, at least you are getting addicted to self-publishing).

Only a few people know that books have almost the longest life span of all products. As mentioned in other chapters The Alchemist and all the Harry Potter books sell thousands of copies every day, even though they first appeared in 1988 and 1997!

In a sense, writing a book is investing in the future. The only problem is that we don't always make our books visible to the crowd. Book marketing is a long game, but after you're done with one book, you will begin on another and, finally, the **synergy** appears. You will sell more copies of your old books as a result of your new books, and your new books will have more sales thanks to your previous books. **Everything is connected.**

Have you ever wondered about your book's rights? Once your book first appears on Amazon you own all the rights, all territorial rights, all languages, and all formats. When you are signing with a publishing house you lend part of these rights out (never give any rights away without any defined time limitation, like 3-5 years). There are three big languages - English, Chinese, and Spanish. You could sell a lot of books just by signing with a new publisher.

DAY 95-100

THE CHECKLIST

This is a point where we can evaluate our marketing efforts, find our weaknesses, and work on them in the following week.

- **Reviews on Amazon**
    1. <5 – Should be improved
    2. 5-20 – Ok
    3. >20 – Excellent
- **Reviews on Goodreads**
    1. <5 – Should be improved
    2. 5-50 – Ok
    3. 50-100 – Very good
    4. >100 – Excellent
- **Amazon Sponsored Ads campaign's ACoS**
    1. >50 – Stop campaign, evaluate keywords and re-launch
    2. 50-25 – Check keywords, stop the ones that are not working, add new ones
    3. 25-15 – Good, you may enter new keywords, and check bids
    4. <15 – Excellent, check bids
- **Amazon Best Sellers Rank**, reflecting on your sales numbers

1. >1,000,000 – There is plenty of marketing work ahead
2. 500,000-1,000,000 – You finally have some sales, but continue with marketing efforts
3. 250,000-500,000 – This is an ideal
4. 100,000-250,000 – Really good, well done!
5. <100,000 – Excellent, you have a lot of sales, now target to get under 10,000 and top 100 in several Amazon Best Sellers category

- **Articles' number** on your website (blog), where you promote your book constantly
    1. <5 – Start writing to rank your website and get higher on Google
    2. 5-10 – Fairly good
    3. 10-20 – Good, you are on track
    4. >20 – Excellent
- **Amazon book's list page**
    1. You have listed your book to all available (8) categories and it is visible on Amazon
    2. You use rich (HTML) formatting in your book's description (bold, italic, listing)
    3. You have a personal, friendly author's bio
    4. You have at least 5 editorial reviews on the book's sales page

DAY 95-100

5. You have a professional author photo uploaded to Amazon Author Central

If you score highly on the above list, then your book has achieved reached its goal and it was worth writing it.

SUMMARIZING 3 YEARS OF MARKETING EXPERIENCE

In the last month (April 2020) we passed the 1000th successful marketing delivery. This means we saw approximately 1,000 books in the last two years and up to 1,500 books in the last four.

We mostly meet with self-published books, but there is no significant difference in how we handle professionally edited books from a marketing perspective. They both deserve attention no matter who wrote or edited the book.

As an extension of this book, we decided to share our experiences. What could be the difference between a well-selling book (Amazon Best Sellers Rank <50,000) and a "zero sold copy" book?

Here is our shortlist:

- Cover
- Amazon blurb and title
- Pricing strategy
- Length of the book
- Understanding of the importance of pre-order state

- Selling books on a website

COMMON MISTAKES RELATED TO BOOKS

COVER

One common mistake among self-published books, that the author doesn't put enough effort into the cover design.

On KDP, there is a Cover Creator tool, which uses some well-known fonts and templates. In 2% of our cases, we meet with these covers and we fail instantly. We fail as marketeers since our job is to sell these books, but we can't. People don't click on unprofessional covers. This is a rough reality.

But it wouldn't be a problem at all; covers are just covers, and we can change them at the end of the day. On KDP we can swap the cover on a weekly basis if we wish to. We often suggest authors to periodically change or try out alternative covers. The problem comes when we receive the answer "I like the current one." Well, this is the main problem, not that the first cover is unprofessional. **You shouldn't stick to any cover ever!**

If you will write more than three books in your lifetime, you will learn this lesson, but first-time authors easily fall in this trap.

If you check any of the best seller books, you will notice, that they have alternate covers for different formats (paperback, Kindle, and audiobook). That's not because they have bigger budget, but the publisher wants to offer something new when you buy a new format and of course, they want to know which cover converts better.

A cover isn't the cheapest part of the book, it may cost from $40 to $3,000, but typically $350.

Never buy a cover concept, buy the time of the designer. A great designer will most likely produce even a better quality cover in his or her worst days than a non-professional in his or her good days. If you find a good designer, stick to him or her, and never let a great partner go.

Now back to covers. There are trends and new styles every year; you can ask the designer to apply these in your new cover, but it won't be a deciding factor when it comes to the reader. The reader will search for that "impression", which makes him or her to click on that cover. Sometimes this could be a color, a memory from childhood, a strange set, or simply something that we have never seen before.

We (as readers) are never searching for uniqueness, but we are searching for **feelings**. Don't try to make a cover with the designer that is unique, but a cover which raises emotions even if it is black and white. This is why stock photos aren't ideal for covers, there are no honest feelings on those pictures. Capturing an honest feeling requires people to experience them, which is almost impossible behind an artificial set.

During my work with professional cover designers I would share some tips with you:

- Never try to tell the designer what exactly should be on the cover, never kill the creativity at the start!
- Tell him ideas, sets, feelings- not expectations.
- Ask three drafts and go with the one which is the closest to your ideas.
- Give time. Designers require inspiration, so when you are talking about your story with passion, it will help him.
- Let him polish the final work, this is the time when he will add all the design parts that will make the cover stand out.

AMAZON BLURB AND TITLE

A lot of self-publishing author understand the importance of the book's description, so they spend some bucks to let a professional create a "converting" blurb for them. Which is a good thing; sometimes an outsider could describe the topic much easier. It is copywriting task after all.

What happens afterward?

The author simply copy-paste the received text into KDP platform and the result is terrible. No line breaks, no formatting, no bullet points, just "text." **Formatting is as important as the content itself.** A lot of readers simply don't start reading text which isn't formatted. And this is a huge problem for the book. We lost a potential reader just because of formatting.

A second typical mistake is with CAPITAL letters. Don't use them! It is like shouting with words, it hurts the eyes. Readers aren't idiots; they know it is a title and an author name. If you want to emphasize something in the description, simply use **bold** text or *italic*. More elegant and more effective. In KDP you can use simple HTML markup, including bullet points.

Another good practice, which I see less and less, is using the subtitle as "keyword" holder, which works really good actually, in terms of Amazon SEO. As the subtitle of the book "What the Wind Knows" should be "A historical romance." This trick could really help in terms of ranking your book for specific search terms on

Amazon. Of course, there are a lot of factors, but this way your main keyword "historical romance" will be present in the title. Never miss this opportunity as a self-published author.

PRICING STRATEGY

We've seen a new trend in the last years, that Kindle books' price is about $10.99-$19.99 for bestselling novels. It isn't cheap at all.

Several weeks earlier — and it isn't a onetime experience — we received a 40 pages short book (non-illustrated) from a first-time author. The Kindle book's price tag was $12.99.

Now this is the situation when we (marketing experts) couldn't do a thing to help the book succeed. It will fail. **Overpricing a book is a big mistake.**

Let me show you how readers are thinking:

1. They see a book cover on the internet; they find the story or the genre fitting with their interest, — they are in the mood to read something similar — so they click on the link.
2. The next thing they will see is the book's Amazon page. They check the book formats, the cover and then, finally, the price tag. Their first

decision is that buying the book is "out of my budget" or isn't.
3. If it isn't, they will check the blurb. Still interested? Let's see some reviews, but before that they check the length (see later) of the book.
4. Reviews and length are ok, the book is worth the price, let's decide "Do I really need this book?"

The process looks really straightforward, but your book needs to climb a lot of ladders to get into cart.

Now let's see the **factors** that should be considered during the creation of pricing strategy:

Are you a famous author?

If you are a first-time author and you aren't a television celebrity, overpricing your book could be very dangerous. It is a fact that reputation matters amongst readers, and your name will mean nothing to the majority. Don't worry- 99% of authors are in the same situation.

From this point the question: "Is your book trendy?" and reviews become an important factor. Nobody cares whether they are positive or negative, just **the count** of the reviews (of course if you have one negative review it is a stop sign).

Books with zero reviews are considered "nobody reads it." We experience this in case of Amazon Ads. If somebody starts a campaign for a brand-new book with no reviews, the impressions and clicks simply won't convert. **Never start a paid ad for your book if you have no reviews.**

Books with 2-5 reviews are considered new books; in this case, readers often check the age of the book. If it is a new release, then 2-5 reviews could be ok, but if the book was released five years ago then it could quickly get into the above category.

Books with 10-25 reviews are considered "could be good" books. In this case, the other factors of the book like the cover, topic, and blurb will be the deciding factor for the purchase decision.

Books above 100 reviews are considered popular books and books that have 1,000+ reviews are considered bestsellers. It is even interesting that people don't like to review the first three category only books that are already popular enough. Nobody wants to be a first-time reviewer unless the book comes from a celebrity writer.

The length of the book

Short books should receive different price tags than books that are above 300+ pages. We all know that everything depends on the quality, but readers don't have the chance to check the quality before the purchase and reviews often don't reflect the quality. So, these readers' control factor will be the length.

Under 100 pages every book considered a short-book. Between 100 and 150 pages the paperback copies are still considered as short-books.

Above 200 pages, we may call a book a normal book. In the case of science fiction (and some other genres) this is 250-300 pages at least.

The average length of the books became shorter over the last ten years. I barely meet with books above 300 pages, self-published authors reduced the average length of the books drastically. Today it is about 120-150 pages.

There is a hidden rule amongst readers-they don't want to pay over $10 for a short book, not even if it's comes from a famous author. There are a lot of alarming issues with length, but in terms of price, readers think that length and price have a correlation.

Age of the book

We often advise self-publishers to keep the Kindle's price low till the book receives 5-10 reviews, simply because we want to keep the "let's try this book out" factor in the hat at the beginning. A lot of people commit impulse purchases—that's a fact—, but they do it once the price is low so to say it is "cheap", which is $0.99-$2.99 in case of Kindle books.

In the first months of the book keep the book's price low. Every read, every purchase may help in the future success of the book.

After we reached 10 reviews the situation changes, slightly. Now our book isn't a newborn, it is a toddler.

This is the time when we (marketeers) simply search for the book title on Amazon, to get informed about the state of the book. If we find only the Amazon link, then we are sure the book requires more exposure. It should appear on websites and articles if we want to make it succeed.

Remember, reviews aren't worth a penny if the book isn't on a book club's website or in articles. People find new titles primarily on third party websites. This is why we could find a lot of fiction book articles on Forbes like "The Best Thrillers of 2019-2020." They know that the popularity of their brand and their website could literally sell **anything**, and not, at last, their website has a really strong SEO present on Google.

Another "age" metric is the book's *"Amazon SEO score"*, which is an invisible number and consists of such metrics as Amazon Best Sellers Rank. This *Amazon SEO score* decides how our book ranks in search results for certain keywords typed in Amazon search bar. This is something we want to build up during the book's lifetime. If we score better our sales will go up. In this case, we consider the book also "aged."

How to determine the final price of my book?

Kindle (e-book) book pricing strategies:

1. $0.99-2.99
   a. Self-published titles
   b. Short books (under 100 pages)
   c. Newly released titles with 0-5 reviews
2. $3.99-4.99
   a. Books in length 150-200 pages
   b. Aged books with 6-15 reviews
   c. The book is listed for certain keywords in the first two pages of Amazon search result
3. $5.99-9.99
   a. Book's length is at least 200 pages
   b. Aged books with 15+ reviews
   c. First-page result for certain keywords
4. $10.99-15.99
   a. Bestseller novels
   b. The author is famous
   c. Aged books with 50+ reviews

d. First-page result for popular keywords on Amazon

Paperback book pricing strategies:

1. $4.99-8.99
    a. Books between 80-150 pages
    b. New self-published titles
    c. No, or few (0-5) reviews
2. $9.99-12.99
    a. Books over 200 pages
    b. Aged books that rank for certain keywords on Amazon
    c. Review count is between 10-20
3. $13.99-$16.99
    a. Books over 300 pages
    b. Aged books that rank first page for certain keywords
    c. Review count is more than 25
4. $17.99-$25.99
    a. Long books and scientific works (400+ pages)
    b. Review count is more than 60

LENGTH OF THE BOOK

People consider non-illustrated books under 50 pages a scam. Not a short book, but a **scam**. I mean everybody could write a "couple of pages" and put it on Amazon in 2020. In the case of short books, you need to convince people:

- Your book doesn't want to hide the fact that it is a short read (strange to say but it isn't obvious)
- Your book has the value to readers even if it is short
- Your book is well-edited, and the necessary effort has been put into it
- Your book is better than 80% of short books, no matter if it is a fiction or non-fiction (so cover and reviews have an important role here)

The biggest mistake in the case of short books is that self-publishers forget to clearly show readers it is a "short read." It will take only two hours to read it. These categories ("30 minutes read", "two-hour read") exist on Amazon. Furthermore, they are an important part of the site.

You need to target your story well. If you want to give value to readers, you should exactly know what your book "gives" to readers. What is the key feature of the story?

People will most likely check the first pages of the book. The inner cover and the first pages will be the deciding factor at this point.

THE IMPORTANCE OF PRE-ORDER STATE

Pre-order state for self-publishers isn't about doing actual sales. It is a myth, and this is why:

- People don't know your name.
- People have a blurb (but often it is barely formatted or says nothing about the book and story).
- People don't know anything about your book's length.
- Your book has zero reviews.

Readers don't buy promises. "Hey, this will be a good book, buy me." Won't work.

On Kickstarter people spend weeks (if not months) polishing a welcome page. They create videos, creatives, models, just only to support the story they want to sell to the visitors (supporters). An Amazon page couldn't produce such a rich experience at the moment.

However, we do emphasize to put your book into pre-order on Amazon with a proper cover (even if it isn't the final cover). Why?

Every marketing act is part of a bigger picture. You tell your friends that you are writing a story. They say ok, can I check it? In most cases, you are saying "I'm sorry it isn't ready yet."

Bad answer.

You should say: "Of course, I will send you the Amazon link!"

Link sent, and your friend will click on it. If it isn't overpriced, he or she may also pre-order it.

A Pre-order link is something we could refer to. It is a physical presence on the web, at least from a marketing perspective. It is "touchable" and the best part that this presence raises the chance to get those first impressions. Because nobody buys anything based on one impression.

This book that you are holding at the moment received 2-3 pre-orders over 2-3 months. I didn't stress about it, because it brought me a lot of value just that I could point to a link on the web. And here comes the trick. Amazon doesn't allow us to review books in pre-order, no matter if anybody received an ARC. But Goodreads does!

You can create a Goodreads link too based on your pre-order book. Most likely it has already an ISBN or at least an ASIN…. more than enough. Now your book is on Goodreads.

One of our customers reported that after he put his book out to Goodreads and sent out several friends an ARC, he received let's say 4-5 reviews on Goodreads. What happened after? People saw the book on Goodreads, they liked the cover, maybe also the blurb. They not only checked in "I want to read," but there were also some cases where reviews were submitted (1-2). This is how the buzz happens.

COMMON MISTAKES RELATED TO ADVERTISING

UNREALISTIC EXPECTATIONS

One of our biggest problems as marketeers is that we need to educate authors on what to expect with certain marketing actions. The first question that appears in our partners:

"If I order your service, how many books will be sold?"

There are many cases when we don't even receive the link of our partner's book.

Well, our basic answer is for the above question is **zero to 100+** with the same ($50) marketing service. Readers are all individuals; they do **choose** books. As a marketeer, our job is to create the opportunity for readers to meet the new book.

As described earlier the decision will be made on the book's Amazon page based on the cover, blurb, reviews, overall quality, and how good it matches with the interest of the reader.

As a marketeer we have no control over these; the best thing we can do is to give advice and tips to authors and publishers.

Self-publishers have certainly a disadvantage in terms of marketing. Bigger publishing houses have their own marketing channels and they have no problem spending up to $10,000 for marketing a "success book." They usually do the same marketing actions for every book (to get the initial reviews and make some exposure for the new release). But remember, we are speaking about traditional publishing houses. Self-publishing agencies usually don't spend any penny on marketing; after they publish your book on Amazon the job is done. They don't care what happens with the book afterward and they know that **80% of books will sell under 100 copies in their lifetime**.

We also don't like the term "free marketing." Nothing is free. Maybe you don't need to pay money directly for listing a book on different websites, but it takes **time. Your time**. Which couldn't be spent on writing your next book.

Back to marketing. As a self-publisher the best thing you can do is to plan a budget for marketing, e.g. $200-300. Forget ROI (return of investment) because every marketing action is for the future. The next year's sales could be the result of this year's "unsuccessful" marketing action. You couldn't evaluate actions individually, but you can follow the sales. This is why we recommend **doing diverse small actions in many places on the web for your book**. Don't spend your budget in one place, but spend in many places.

AMAZON ADS

You couldn't run Amazon Ads for every book genre

Some of our partners aren't aware that Amazon Ads have many restrictions in terms of what it allows to be promoted.

There are several prohibited book niches like:

- Adult romance books (Erotica or explicit sexuality)
- Alcohol, Drugs, Tobago related books
- Financial products, cryptocurrencies or any financial services

- Advocating or demeaning any religion
- Medical treatment, drug-related books, or books claiming to cure any physical or mental diseases

This makes a lot of confusion among authors whose books are actually in the above niches since the problem turns out once the book's marketing campaign is rejected and already a lot of effort spent to set up the campaign.

In the resources section, we put the link of the Amazon Ads acceptance policy in order to avoid any awkward moments with Amazon Ads.

Keywords

We see that people tend to pay $50-100 for keyword tools like Publisher Rocket and they simply copy-paste keywords directly into their AAP (Amazon Advertising Platform) campaign. Keywords tools are useful if we also add our own common-sense knowledge to it.

Generally, in a 200-300 keywords campaigns 90% of the keywords are trash:

- They are too generic and won't bring enough sales in the long term
- They are not connected directly to the book's topic, or readers couldn't connect their keyword to the book based on the title, blurb or cover (for example if somebody is looking for a YA fantasy

book, but our cover and blurb doesn't reflect the genre specifics)

In general, I would say 40-50 well targeted and specific keywords should be enough for a successful Amazon Ads campaign.

Conversion rate

Another typical mistake is to start an Amazon ad too early after the book launch. **No, it isn't the way for collecting the first reviews.**

We need to build up trust with the book's Amazon page in the potential readers. An almost blank page, a book cover, some lines of description with no reviews won't do the job if you want your paid ad to convert.

A lot of people don't realize that you could put a lot of things on to the book's Amazon page. We bolded the items that 75% of self-publishers forget about:

1. Cover
2. Title
3. **Subtitle** (which requires holding the most important keyword(s) about the book)
4. Description or blurb
5. **Author bio**
6. **Editorial reviews**
7. **From author section**

8. Reviews

Our first job after the launch should be to take the time and upload content to all of the above sections and ask our friends and relatives to review our book (they most likely bought it anyway).

Several of the above sections aren't available in Amazon Seller Central or KDP, but you will find them in Amazon Author Central which has a lot of new functions in 2020.

If we do the above steps and we collected the first 5-10 reviews, we may launch an Amazon Advertising campaign.

QUALITY OF MARKETING VISUALS

If you have an Instagram or a Facebook page, and you want to present your new book to your audience, you will definitely use some kind of visual creative.

Most of the authors come up with the idea to hire a designer to create a 3D mockup from his book's cover because it converts. This is a myth, **mockup creatives don't convert better than traditional photos**. In fact great quality photos receive more likes than mockups (e.g. on Instagram).

The main problems with these mockups:

- The quality of cover used for creating the mockup wasn't sufficient so the outcome will be barely readable
- They don't feel realistic at all
- They are too standard, almost the same angle
- Their background is stuffed with text

What do I suggest?

Don't use mockups, **use real photos**! Today's mobile devices have excellent cameras. **With proper lighting, we can create sharp quality pictures**.

Don't stress about the background; there is absolutely no problem if it doesn't match perfectly with the book's message. Use nature, use places which give **you** positive feelings. Take your book into your own hand. Focus more on the contrast — use a different color for the background than the cover's main color—, and the sharpness of the photo.

After you took several photos, just pick your favorite, and use it as a Facebook or Instagram post. If you have any message to the readers just put it into the post, not on the picture. You will see the difference in response rate.

BOOK GENRES

It is a myth that every book has the same chance of success. With choosing your book's topic, you do lose a huge group of people.

As we already told you, we were enough lucky to meet with up to 1,000 titles, in the past years. And truth to be told we have some very rough time marketing some niches.

For example, marketing a general fiction book with Amazon Ads is a nightmare. You could find only generic keywords, which don't convert and it is a waste of money for the author. So here it is our shortlist, of book genres which are very hard to market:

- Poetry books - Poetry has a very limited audience in 2020; younger generations don't tend to read these titles. They are reflecting the experience to the authors and from the readers' perspective it is one of the hardest readable works. Autobiographies are working in a sense much better when we think about readability.
- Success books – Success is relative, and these books are only bestsellers if it is written by a celebrity or well-known authors. On the other side, there is a huge competition in this genre.

- Diet or cookbooks – There is extremely big competition in this genre. No matter if you are writing a paleo, plant only, vegan or any other cookbook in this genre, the problem is the same. People are searching for recipes on the internet and looking less for books.
- Children's books – There are a pro and con in this genre. It is easy to promote a children's book that has quality graphics and it is extremely hard if the visuals are from an amateur or semi-amateur graphic designer. People check the first pages of these books, and they buy the book, only if they like visual outlook.
- Personal success books – It is one of the most competitive niches among non-fiction books. This category isn't just present in business but also in the biography and memoir niche. Success is a psychological experience, and as an author, it is really hard to find the essence of it. For marketers the situation is similar. Writing the success in the title makes the book ten times harder to sell, this is why the best selling authors never do that.
- Financial freedom books – Financials are highly sensitive topics for most people. Unless the author has good references and an extensive author profile on Amazon, it is almost

impossible to market these books. For authors in this genre, strong credibility is essential. Nobody will trust in your book if you won't even put out an author photo of you.

But let's see the other end, which are books that is easy to market:

- YA Fantasy – This is an emerging niche, but not too many people are working on it, mostly younger writers. A good cover and a story could end up in many sales.
- Programming books – We had several success stories in this genre, these books have their own keywords which could be used on Amazon Ads easily, and they do convert.
- Thrillers – We found that there is a strong need for thriller books: psychological thrillers, techno-thriller, spy thrillers, robot or futuristic thrillers, crime thrillers, etc. People love kick-ass stories, where the protagonist goes through a lot of dangerous adventures.
- Historical mystery – These books are fitting well in the entertaining category. It is a small but very well-defined genre.
- Social Issues non-fiction – Trends are important, books that connect to these current events have an advantage as it was #BlackLivesMatter

movement in 2020. An exception was the COVID topic, because of other reasons.

- Rom-com – Not every romance book becomes a best seller, simply because there is a huge competition in this genre. This is why sub-genres are important and targeting the story to the right audience. Rom-com is a new light genre that is well defined.

SUMMARY

What we learned from the past years is that marketing is about **dedication**. Perform the essential first steps after the release of the book, like ensuring the book is listed on Goodreads. Improve your book's Amazon page periodically, by updating it with editorial reviews. These small steps mean nothing individually, but together they validate the book and make it stand out from the crowd.

Authors have their own brands, you need to build up also this part, having an email list, a website. Successful authors have more than five books in their lifetime. In marketing one of the most important effect, we are constantly looking at is **synergy**. When one book starts kicking-off the other one will also sell.

Today we don't just sell one story, one book. We need to also sell the author and his own story, the motivation, and the feelings behind it.

Never give up, look always toward to the next step!

I wish you a successful book!
Joel

"Books are valuable only in hands"

If you enjoyed reading this book or you found some important messages in it, don't hesitate to give it to a friend.

Author's note

This is a self-published book. I choose this form of publication because I deeply believe this is the future. As everything, self-publishing has its drawback at the moment, readers rely more on reviews, so if you could give any feedback to this book on Goodreads or Amazon, it would be a great help!

If you would like to contact the author feel free to email to joel@joelbooks.com

Printed in Great Britain
by Amazon